The First Steps in Education Last a Lifetime

Join Our Team
Achieve a Dream
Knowledge Changes You
You Change the World

SMARTGRADES
BRAIN POWER REVOLUTION

We Empower Students for
Academic Success in School,
Personal Success at Home, and
Professional Success at Work

www.smartgrades.com

©2007-2024

This book is not an orphan. If lost, please return to:

Name: ___________________________________

School: __________________________________

Grade: ___________________________________

SMARTGRADES Class Schedule

MONDAY	Class	Room#	Time	Teacher Name
1st Class				
2nd Class				
3rd Class				
4th Class				
5th Class				

TUESDAY	Class	Room#	Time	Teacher Name
1st Class				
2nd Class				
3rd Class				
4th Class				
5th Class				

WEDNESDAY	Class	Room#	Time	Teacher Name
1st Class				
2nd Class				
3rd Class				
4th Class				
5th Class				

THURSDAY	Class	Room#	Time	Teacher Name
1st Class				
2nd Class				
3rd Class				
4th Class				
5th Class				

FRIDAY	Class	Room#	Time	Teacher Name
1st Class				
2nd Class				
3rd Class				
4th Class				
5th Class				

DAILY HABITS DAILY REWARDS

What's Inside?

- Class Schedule Planner
- Academic Calendar Planner
- In Class: Homework Assignment Planner
- At Home: Study Schedule Planner
- Setting Priorities Tracker
- Time Management Tracker
- Practice: Gratitude Is Happiness
- Practice: Positive Self-Talk
- Practice: Random Act of Kindness
- Practice: Building Good Character Traits
- Practice: Meditation to Reduce Stress and Anxiety
- Menu Planner
- Budget and Expense Tracker: Save, Spend, and Spurge
- After-School Activities Planner
- Family Chores Planner
- Self-Reflection Journal
- Grade Tracker: Good Grades Deserve Great Rewards!
- Teacher Contacts
- Study Buddy Contacts
- Regular Bedtime Planner
- PHOTON SUPERHERO Positive Self-Talk Affirmations
- PHOTON SUPERHERO 22 Spiritual Illuminations
- PHOTON SUPERHERO 10 Facts of Academic Success
- PHOTON SUPERHERO Time Management Tips

Academic Calendar: August-January

Class	What's Due?	Due Date
August	❑ Back to School Preparation	

September

October

November

December

January

Academic Calendar: February-June

Class	What's Due?	Due Date
February		

March

April

May

June

In Class: My Homework Assignments

Today's Date:

1st Assignment
Class/Subject: _ _ _ _ _ _ _ _ _ _ _ _ _
Due Date:

Priority# _ _ _
Estimate Time: _ _ _
Actual Time: _ _ _
❑ Test-Review Notes?
❑ Proofreading Help?
❑ Tutoring Help?

2nd Assignment
Class/Subject: _ _ _ _ _ _ _ _ _ _ _ _ _
Due Date:

Priority# _ _ _
Estimate Time: _ _ _
Actual Time: _ _ _
❑ Test-Review Notes?
❑ Proofreading Help?
❑ Tutoring Help?

3rd Assignment
Class/Subject: _ _ _ _ _ _ _ _ _ _ _ _ _
Due Date:

Priority# _ _ _
Estimate Time: _ _ _
Actual Time: _ _ _
❑ Test-Review Notes?
❑ Proofreading Help?
❑ Tutoring Help?

4th Assignment
Class/Subject: _ _ _ _ _ _ _ _ _ _ _ _ _
Due Date:

Priority# _ _ _
Estimate Time: _ _ _
Actual Time: _ _ _
❑ Test-Review Notes?
❑ Proofreading Help?
❑ Tutoring Help?

5th Assignment
Class/Subject: _ _ _ _ _ _ _ _ _ _ _ _ _
Due Date:

Priority# _ _ _
Estimate Time: _ _ _
Actual Time: _ _ _
❑ Test-Review Notes?
❑ Proofreading Help?
❑ Tutoring Help?

6th Assignment
Class/Subject: _ _ _ _ _ _ _ _ _ _ _ _ _
Due Date:

Priority# _ _ _
Estimate Time: _ _ _
Actual Time: _ _ _
❑ Test-Review Notes?
❑ Proofreading Help?
❑ Tutoring Help?

At Home: My Study Schedule

7 Shift Study Schedule
45-Minute Study Periods and 15-Minute Breaks

Study Period 1
3-3:45   Subject: __________
15 Minute Study Break (stretch)

Study Period 2
4-4:45   Subject: __________
15 Minute Study Break (stretch)

Study Period 3
5-5:45   Subject:__________
15 Minute Study Break (stretch)

Study Period 4
6-6:45   Subject:__________
15 Minute Study Break (stretch)

Study Period 5
7-7:45   Subject:__________
15 Minute Study Break (stretch)

Study Period 6
8-8:45   Subject:__________
15 Minute Study Break (stretch)

Study Period 7
9-9:45   Subject: __________
15 Minutes: Pack Book Bag for Tomorrow

Regular Bedtime for Energy to Learn

Get Ready for Tomorrow!

❑ 1. Pack Book Bag
❑ 2. Check: Keys, School I.D., Wallet, Money, Pens and Pencils, Assignments
❑ 3. Check Weather (Umbrella? Snow Boots? Sunscreen?)
❑ 4. Q. What Will You Eat for Breakfast and Lunch Tomorrow?
❑ 5. Q. What Will You Wear to School Tomorrow?
❑ 6. Charge Electronic Devices (Computer, Cell Phone, and Watch)
❑ 7. Express Gratitude to Loved Ones (Hugs & Kisses, Love Note, Gift)
❑ 8. Brush & Floss Teeth
❑ 9. Set Alarm Clock

Set Priorities:

Priority #1
❑ Prepare EZ Study Snacks
   e.g., Apple Slices, Banana,
   Celery & Carrot Sticks

Priority #2
Q. What Time Is Dinner?

Priority #3
❑ Study Period #1
   Study for Test!

Priority #4
❑ Study Period #2
   What's Due Tomorrow?

Priority #5
❑ What's Due Next Week?

Priority #6
❑ Write Test-Review Notes
   to Ace Tests:
   1. Class Notes
   2. Textbook Notes
   3. Handout Notes

Priority #7
❑ Review Test-Review
   Notes to Ace Tests

Priority #8
❑ Write Essays and
   Research Reports
❑ Proofreading Help?

Priority #9
❑ Tutoring Help?

Priority #10
❑ Backup Computer

Priority #11
❑ Pack Book Bag

Priority #12
❑ Socialize with
   Family & Friends
   Time: 8-9 p.m.

Priority #13
❑ Stick to a Regular
   Bedtime: 9-11 p.m.

My Daily Self-Care Journal

1. Practice Gratitude:
   I am grateful for...

----

2. Practice Positive Self-Talk:
   I am ...

----

3. Practice Meditation:
   Close your eyes for 1-5 minutes, and pay attention to your breathing.
   Focus your mind on your breathing to become centered and calmer.

----

4. My Healthy Food Energy Choices:

   Breakfast Energy: _______________________________________

   Lunch Energy: ____

   Dinner Energy: ____

   Study Snack Energy: ___________________________________

   Eat Whole Foods of Fresh Fruits and Vegetables. Minimize Processed Food and Junk Food.

----

5. My Budget: Save, Spend, and Splurge

Part 1. My Budget

Total Amount of Allowance & Earnings: $ ________ Budget

1. My Savings: Pay Yourself First! $ ________ Savings Bank Account

2. My Pocket Money $ ________ My Wallet

Part 2. My Expenses: Needs & Wants

1. Spend (My Needs): $ ________

2. Splurge (My Wants): $ ________

Total Expenses: $ ________

Part 3.
My Pocket Money Minus My Expenses = $ ________ Balance

6. My After-School Activity:

____

7. My Family Chores:

1.

2.

3.

____

8. A Random Act of Kindness:
I made a difference in someone else's life by...

____

9. Self-Reflection

❑ Great Day   ❑ Good Day   ❑ Bad Day

1. The Best Part of My Day:

----

2. The Worst Part of My Day:

----

3. How Can I Become a Better Person Tomorrow?

4. Did You Put LOVE Into Everything?

----

5. What Is the Stress Level at Home? _______ (#1-10)

6. What Is the Stress Level at School? _______ (#1-10)

____

Practice Building
Good Character Traits

1. Courage
2. Responsibility
3. Kindness
4. Optimisim
5. Loyalty
6. Confidence
7. Honesty
8. Compassion
9. Cooperation
10. Open-Minded
11. Keep Your Word
12. Respectful Communication
13. Courtesy
14. Fair Play

10. ENERGIZE

My Regular Bedtime for POPTART ENERGY Is: _______ p.m.

In Class: My Homework Assignments

Today's Date:

1st Assignment
Class/Subject: _____________
Due Date:

Priority# ___
Estimate Time: ___
Actual Time: ___
❑ Test-Review Notes?
❑ Proofreading Help?
❑ Tutoring Help?

2nd Assignment
Class/Subject: _____________
Due Date:

Priority# ___
Estimate Time: ___
Actual Time: ___
❑ Test-Review Notes?
❑ Proofreading Help?
❑ Tutoring Help?

3rd Assignment
Class/Subject: _____________
Due Date:

Priority# ___
Estimate Time: ___
Actual Time: ___
❑ Test-Review Notes?
❑ Proofreading Help?
❑ Tutoring Help?

4th Assignment
Class/Subject: _____________
Due Date:

Priority# ___
Estimate Time: ___
Actual Time: ___
❑ Test-Review Notes?
❑ Proofreading Help?
❑ Tutoring Help?

5th Assignment
Class/Subject: _____________
Due Date:

Priority# ___
Estimate Time: ___
Actual Time: ___
❑ Test-Review Notes?
❑ Proofreading Help?
❑ Tutoring Help?

6th Assignment
Class/Subject: _____________
Due Date:

Priority# ___
Estimate Time: ___
Actual Time: ___
❑ Test-Review Notes?
❑ Proofreading Help?
❑ Tutoring Help?

At Home: My Study Schedule

7 Shift Study Schedule
45-Minute Study Periods and 15-Minute Breaks

Study Period 1
3-3:45   Subject: __________
15 Minute Study Break (stretch)

Study Period 2
4-4:45   Subject: __________
15 Minute Study Break (stretch)

Study Period 3
5-5:45   Subject:__________
15 Minute Study Break (stretch)

Study Period 4
6-6:45   Subject:__________
15 Minute Study Break (stretch)

Study Period 5
7-7:45   Subject:__________
15 Minute Study Break (stretch)

Study Period 6
8-8:45   Subject:__________
15 Minute Study Break (stretch)

Study Period 7
9-9:45   Subject: __________
15 Minutes: Pack Book Bag for Tomorrow

Regular Bedtime for Energy to Learn

Get Ready for Tomorrow!

❑ 1. Pack Book Bag
❑ 2. Check: Keys, School I.D., Wallet, Money, Pens and Pencils, Assignments
❑ 3. Check Weather (Umbrella? Snow Boots? Sunscreen?)
❑ 4. Q. What Will You Eat for Breakfast and Lunch Tomorrow?
❑ 5. Q. What Will You Wear to School Tomorrow?
❑ 6. Charge Electronic Devices (Computer, Cell Phone, and Watch)
❑ 7. Express Gratitude to Loved Ones (Hugs & Kisses, Love Note, Gift)
❑ 8. Brush & Floss Teeth
❑ 9. Set Alarm Clock

Set Priorities:

Priority #1
❑ Prepare **EZ** Study Snacks
e.g., Apple Slices, Banana,
Celery & Carrot Sticks

Priority #2
Q. What Time Is Dinner?

Priority #3
❑ Study Period #1
Study for Test!

Priority #4
❑ Study Period #2
What's Due Tomorrow?

Priority #5
❑ What's Due Next Week?

Priority #6
❑ Write Test-Review Notes
to Ace Tests:
1. Class Notes
2. Textbook Notes
3. Handout Notes

Priority #7
❑ Review Test-Review
Notes to Ace Tests

Priority #8
❑ Write Essays and
Research Reports
❑ Proofreading Help?

Priority #9
❑ Tutoring Help?

Priority #10
❑ Backup Computer

Priority #11
❑ Pack Book Bag

Priority #12
❑ Socialize with
Family & Friends
Time: 8-9 p.m.

Priority #13
❑ Stick to a Regular
Bedtime: 9-11 p.m.

My Daily Self-Care Journal

1. Practice Gratitude:
   I am grateful for...

----

2. Practice Positive Self-Talk:
   I am ...

----

3. Practice Meditation:
   Close your eyes for 1-5 minutes, and pay attention to your breathing.
   Focus your mind on your breathing to become centered and calmer.

----

4. My Healthy Food Energy Choices:

   Breakfast Energy: ____

   Lunch Energy: ____

   Dinner Energy: ____

   Study Snack Energy: _____________________________________

   Eat Whole Foods of Fresh Fruits and Vegetables. Minimize Processed Food and Junk Food.

----

5. My Budget: Save, Spend, and Splurge

Part 1. My Budget

Total Amount of Allowance & Earnings: $ ________ Budget

1. My Savings: Pay Yourself First! $ ________ Savings Bank Account

2. My Pocket Money $ ________ My Wallet

Part 2. My Expenses: Needs & Wants

1. Spend (My Needs): $ ________

2. Splurge (My Wants): $ ________

Total Expenses: $ ________

Part 3.
My Pocket Money Minus My Expenses = $ ________ Balance

6. My After-School Activity:

____

7. My Family Chores:

    1.

    2.

    3.

____

8. A Random Act of Kindness:
   I made a difference in someone else's life by...

____

9. Self-Reflection

❑ Great Day   ❑ Good Day   ❑ Bad Day

1. The Best Part of My Day:

----

2. The Worst Part of My Day:

----

3. How Can I Become a Better Person Tomorrow?

4. Did You Put **LOVE** Into Everything?

----

5. What Is the Stress Level at Home? _______ (#1-10)

6. What Is the Stress Level at School? _______ (#1-10)

____

Practice Building
Good Character Traits

1. Courage
2. Responsibility
3. Kindness
4. Optimisim
5. Loyalty
6. Confidence
7. Honesty
8. Compassion
9. Cooperation
10. Open-Minded
11. Keep Your Word
12. Respectful Communication
13. Courtesy
14. Fair Play

10. ENERGIZE

My Regular Bedtime for POPTART ENERGY Is: ______ p.m.

In Class: My Homework Assignments

Today's Date:

1st Assignment
Class/Subject: _____________
Due Date:

Priority# ___
Estimate Time: ___
Actual Time: ___
❑ Test-Review Notes?
❑ Proofreading Help?
❑ Tutoring Help?

2nd Assignment
Class/Subject: _____________
Due Date:

Priority# ___
Estimate Time: ___
Actual Time: ___
❑ Test-Review Notes?
❑ Proofreading Help?
❑ Tutoring Help?

3rd Assignment
Class/Subject: _____________
Due Date:

Priority# ___
Estimate Time: ___
Actual Time: ___
❑ Test-Review Notes?
❑ Proofreading Help?
❑ Tutoring Help?

4th Assignment
Class/Subject: _____________
Due Date:

Priority# ___
Estimate Time: ___
Actual Time: ___
❑ Test-Review Notes?
❑ Proofreading Help?
❑ Tutoring Help?

5th Assignment
Class/Subject: _____________
Due Date:

Priority# ___
Estimate Time: ___
Actual Time: ___
❑ Test-Review Notes?
❑ Proofreading Help?
❑ Tutoring Help?

6th Assignment
Class/Subject: _____________
Due Date:

Priority# ___
Estimate Time: ___
Actual Time: ___
❑ Test-Review Notes?
❑ Proofreading Help?
❑ Tutoring Help?

At Home: My Study Schedule

7 Shift Study Schedule
45-Minute Study Periods and 15-Minute Breaks

Study Period 1
3-3:45   Subject: __________
15 Minute Study Break (stretch)

Study Period 2
4-4:45   Subject: __________
15 Minute Study Break (stretch)

Study Period 3
5-5:45   Subject:__________
15 Minute Study Break (stretch)

Study Period 4
6-6:45   Subject:__________
15 Minute Study Break (stretch)

Study Period 5
7-7:45   Subject:__________
15 Minute Study Break (stretch)

Study Period 6
8-8:45   Subject:__________
15 Minute Study Break (stretch)

Study Period 7
9-9:45   Subject: __________
15 Minutes: Pack Book Bag for Tomorrow

Regular Bedtime for Energy to Learn

Get Ready for Tomorrow!

❑ 1. Pack Book Bag
❑ 2. Check: Keys, School I.D., Wallet, Money, Pens and Pencils, Assignments
❑ 3. Check Weather (Umbrella? Snow Boots? Sunscreen?)
❑ 4. Q. What Will You Eat for Breakfast and Lunch Tomorrow?
❑ 5. Q. What Will You Wear to School Tomorrow?
❑ 6. Charge Electronic Devices (Computer, Cell Phone, and Watch)
❑ 7. Express Gratitude to Loved Ones (Hugs & Kisses, Love Note, Gift)
❑ 8. Brush & Floss Teeth
❑ 9. Set Alarm Clock

Set Priorities:

Priority #1
❑ Prepare **EZ** Study Snacks
e.g., Apple Slices, Banana, Celery & Carrot Sticks

Priority #2
Q. What Time Is Dinner?

Priority #3
❑ Study Period #1
Study for Test!

Priority #4
❑ Study Period #2
What's Due Tomorrow?

Priority #5
❑ What's Due Next Week?

Priority #6
❑ Write Test-Review Notes to Ace Tests:
1. Class Notes
2. Textbook Notes
3. Handout Notes

Priority #7
❑ Review Test-Review Notes to Ace Tests

Priority #8
❑ Write Essays and Research Reports
❑ Proofreading Help?

Priority #9
❑ Tutoring Help?

Priority #10
❑ Backup Computer

Priority #11
❑ Pack Book Bag

Priority #12
❑ Socialize with Family & Friends Time: 8-9 p.m.

Priority #13
❑ Stick to a Regular Bedtime: 9-11 p.m.

My Daily Self-Care Journal

1. **Practice Gratitude:**
   I am grateful for...
   ----

2. **Practice Positive Self-Talk:**
   I am ...
   ----

3. **Practice Meditation:**
   Close your eyes for 1-5 minutes, and pay attention to your breathing.
   Focus your mind on your breathing to become centered and calmer.
   ----

4. **My Healthy Food Energy Choices:**

   Breakfast Energy: ____

   Lunch Energy: ____

   Dinner Energy: ____

   Study Snack Energy: ____

   Eat Whole Foods of Fresh Fruits and Vegetables. Minimize Processed Food and Junk Food.
   ----

5. My Budget: Save, Spend, and Splurge

Part 1. My Budget

Total Amount of Allowance & Earnings: $ ________ Budget

1. My Savings: Pay Yourself First! $ ________ Savings Bank Account

2. My Pocket Money $ ________ My Wallet

Part 2. My Expenses: Needs & Wants

1. Spend (My Needs): $ ________

2. Splurge (My Wants): $ ________

Total Expenses: $ ________

Part 3.
My Pocket Money Minus My Expenses = $ ________ Balance

6. My After-School Activity:

——————————————————————————————————————

7. My Family Chores:

   1.

   2.

   3.

——————————————————————————————————————

8. A Random Act of Kindness:
I made a difference in someone else's life by...

——————————————————————————————————————

9. Self-Reflection

❑ Great Day   ❑ Good Day   ❑ Bad Day

1. The Best Part of My Day:

----

2. The Worst Part of My Day:

----

3. How Can I Become a Better Person Tomorrow?

4. Did You Put **LOVE** Into Everything?

——————————————————————————————————

5. What Is the Stress Level at Home? _______ (#1-10)

6. What Is the Stress Level at School? _______ (#1-10)

——————————————————————————————————————

Practice Building
Good Character Traits

1. Courage
2. Responsibility
3. Kindness
4. Optimisim
5. Loyalty
6. Confidence
7. Honesty
8. Compassion
9. Cooperation
10. Open-Minded
11. Keep Your Word
12. Respectful Communication
13. Courtesy
14. Fair Play

10. ENERGIZE

My Regular Bedtime for POPTART ENERGY Is: _______ p.m.

In Class: My Homework Assignments

Today's Date:

1st Assignment
Class/Subject: _ _ _ _ _ _ _ _ _ _ _ _
Due Date:

Priority# _ _ _
Estimate Time: _ _ _
Actual Time: _ _ _
❏ Test-Review Notes?
❏ Proofreading Help?
❏ Tutoring Help?

2nd Assignment
Class/Subject: _ _ _ _ _ _ _ _ _ _ _ _
Due Date:

Priority# _ _ _
Estimate Time: _ _ _
Actual Time: _ _ _
❏ Test-Review Notes?
❏ Proofreading Help?
❏ Tutoring Help?

3rd Assignment
Class/Subject: _ _ _ _ _ _ _ _ _ _ _ _
Due Date:

Priority# _ _ _
Estimate Time: _ _ _
Actual Time: _ _ _
❏ Test-Review Notes?
❏ Proofreading Help?
❏ Tutoring Help?

4th Assignment
Class/Subject: _ _ _ _ _ _ _ _ _ _ _ _
Due Date:

Priority# _ _ _
Estimate Time: _ _ _
Actual Time: _ _ _
❏ Test-Review Notes?
❏ Proofreading Help?
❏ Tutoring Help?

5th Assignment
Class/Subject: _ _ _ _ _ _ _ _ _ _ _ _
Due Date:

Priority# _ _ _
Estimate Time: _ _ _
Actual Time: _ _ _
❏ Test-Review Notes?
❏ Proofreading Help?
❏ Tutoring Help?

6th Assignment
Class/Subject: _ _ _ _ _ _ _ _ _ _ _ _
Due Date:

Priority# _ _ _
Estimate Time: _ _ _
Actual Time: _ _ _
❏ Test-Review Notes?
❏ Proofreading Help?
❏ Tutoring Help?

At Home: My Study Schedule

7 Shift Study Schedule
45-Minute Study Periods and 15-Minute Breaks

Study Period 1
3-3:45   Subject: __________
15 Minute Study Break (stretch)

Study Period 2
4-4:45   Subject: __________
15 Minute Study Break (stretch)

Study Period 3
5-5:45   Subject:__________
15 Minute Study Break (stretch)

Study Period 4
6-6:45   Subject:__________
15 Minute Study Break (stretch)

Study Period 5
7-7:45   Subject:__________
15 Minute Study Break (stretch)

Study Period 6
8-8:45   Subject:__________
15 Minute Study Break (stretch)

Study Period 7
9-9:45   Subject: __________
15 Minutes: Pack Book Bag for Tomorrow

Regular Bedtime for Energy to Learn

Get Ready for Tomorrow!

❑ 1. Pack Book Bag
❑ 2. Check: Keys, School I.D., Wallet, Money, Pens and Pencils, Assignments
❑ 3. Check Weather (Umbrella? Snow Boots? Sunscreen?)
❑ 4. Q. What Will You Eat for Breakfast and Lunch Tomorrow?
❑ 5. Q. What Will You Wear to School Tomorrow?
❑ 6. Charge Electronic Devices (Computer, Cell Phone, and Watch)
❑ 7. Express Gratitude to Loved Ones (Hugs & Kisses, Love Note, Gift)
❑ 8. Brush & Floss Teeth
❑ 9. Set Alarm Clock

Set Priorities:

Priority #1
❑ Prepare EZ Study Snacks
   e.g., Apple Slices, Banana,
   Celery & Carrot Sticks

Priority #2
Q. What Time Is Dinner?

Priority #3
❑ Study Period #1
   Study for Test!

Priority #4
❑ Study Period #2
   What's Due Tomorrow?

Priority #5
❑ What's Due Next Week?

Priority #6
❑ Write Test-Review Notes
   to Ace Tests:
   1. Class Notes
   2. Textbook Notes
   3. Handout Notes

Priority #7
❑ Review Test-Review
   Notes to Ace Tests

Priority #8
❑ Write Essays and
   Research Reports
❑ Proofreading Help?

Priority #9
❑ Tutoring Help?

Priority #10
❑ Backup Computer

Priority #11
❑ Pack Book Bag

Priority #12
❑ Socialize with
   Family & Friends
   Time: 8-9 p.m.

Priority #13
❑ Stick to a Regular
   Bedtime: 9-11 p.m.

My Daily Self-Care Journal

1. **Practice Gratitude:**
   I am grateful for...
   ----
2. **Practice Positive Self-Talk:**
   I am ...
   ----
3. **Practice Meditation:**
   Close your eyes for 1-5 minutes, and pay attention to your breathing.
   Focus your mind on your breathing to become centered and calmer.
   ----
4. **My Healthy Food Energy Choices:**

   Breakfast Energy: ____

   Lunch Energy: ____

   Dinner Energy: ____

   Study Snack Energy: ____

   Eat Whole Foods of Fresh Fruits and Vegetables. Minimize Processed Food and Junk Food.
   ----

5. My Budget: Save, Spend, and Splurge

Part 1. My Budget

Total Amount of Allowance & Earnings: $ ________ Budget

1. My Savings: Pay Yourself First! $ ________ Savings Bank Account

2. My Pocket Money $ ________ My Wallet

Part 2. My Expenses: Needs & Wants

1. Spend (My Needs): $ ________

2. Splurge (My Wants): $ ________

Total Expenses: $ ________

Part 3.
My Pocket Money Minus My Expenses = $ ________ Balance

6. My After-School Activity:

____

7. My Family Chores:

   1.

   2.

   3.

____

8. A Random Act of Kindness:
   I made a difference in someone else's life by...

____

9. Self-Reflection

❑ Great Day   ❑ Good Day   ❑ Bad Day

1. The Best Part of My Day:

----

2. The Worst Part of My Day:

----

3. How Can I Become a Better Person Tomorrow?

4. Did You Put **LOVE** Into Everything?

____

5. What Is the Stress Level at Home? _______ (#1-10)

6. What Is the Stress Level at School? _______ (#1-10)

____

Practice Building
Good Character Traits

1. Courage
2. Responsibility
3. Kindness
4. Optimisim
5. Loyalty
6. Confidence
7. Honesty
8. Compassion
9. Cooperation
10. Open-Minded
11. Keep Your Word
12. Respectful Communication
13. Courtesy
14. Fair Play

10. ENERGIZE

My Regular Bedtime for POPTART ENERGY Is: _______ p.m.

In Class: My Homework Assignments

Today's Date:

1st Assignment
Class/Subject: _______________
Due Date:

Priority# ___
Estimate Time: ___
Actual Time: ___
❑ Test-Review Notes?
❑ Proofreading Help?
❑ Tutoring Help?

2nd Assignment
Class/Subject: _______________
Due Date:

Priority# ___
Estimate Time: ___
Actual Time: ___
❑ Test-Review Notes?
❑ Proofreading Help?
❑ Tutoring Help?

3rd Assignment
Class/Subject: _______________
Due Date:

Priority# ___
Estimate Time: ___
Actual Time: ___
❑ Test-Review Notes?
❑ Proofreading Help?
❑ Tutoring Help?

4th Assignment
Class/Subject: _______________
Due Date:

Priority# ___
Estimate Time: ___
Actual Time: ___
❑ Test-Review Notes?
❑ Proofreading Help?
❑ Tutoring Help?

5th Assignment
Class/Subject: _______________
Due Date:

Priority# ___
Estimate Time: ___
Actual Time: ___
❑ Test-Review Notes?
❑ Proofreading Help?
❑ Tutoring Help?

6th Assignment
Class/Subject: _______________
Due Date:

Priority# ___
Estimate Time: ___
Actual Time: ___
❑ Test-Review Notes?
❑ Proofreading Help?
❑ Tutoring Help?

At Home: My Study Schedule

7 Shift Study Schedule
45-Minute Study Periods and 15-Minute Breaks

Study Period 1
3-3:45   Subject: __________
15 Minute Study Break (stretch)

Study Period 2
4-4:45   Subject: __________
15 Minute Study Break (stretch)

Study Period 3
5-5:45   Subject:__________
15 Minute Study Break (stretch)

Study Period 4
6-6:45   Subject:__________
15 Minute Study Break (stretch)

Study Period 5
7-7:45   Subject:__________
15 Minute Study Break (stretch)

Study Period 6
8-8:45   Subject:__________
15 Minute Study Break (stretch)

Study Period 7
9-9:45   Subject: __________
15 Minutes: Pack Book Bag for Tomorrow

Regular Bedtime for Energy to Learn

Get Ready for Tomorrow!

❑ 1. Pack Book Bag
❑ 2. Check: Keys, School I.D., Wallet, Money, Pens and Pencils, Assignments
❑ 3. Check Weather (Umbrella? Snow Boots? Sunscreen?)
❑ 4. Q. What Will You Eat for Breakfast and Lunch Tomorrow?
❑ 5. Q. What Will You Wear to School Tomorrow?
❑ 6. Charge Electronic Devices (Computer, Cell Phone, and Watch)
❑ 7. Express Gratitude to Loved Ones (Hugs & Kisses, Love Note, Gift)
❑ 8. Brush & Floss Teeth
❑ 9. Set Alarm Clock

Set Priorities:

Priority #1
❑ Prepare EZ Study Snacks
   e.g., Apple Slices, Banana,
   Celery & Carrot Sticks

Priority #2
Q. What Time Is Dinner?

Priority #3
❑ Study Period #1
   Study for Test!

Priority #4
❑ Study Period #2
   What's Due Tomorrow?

Priority #5
❑ What's Due Next Week?

Priority #6
❑ Write Test-Review Notes
   to Ace Tests:
   1. Class Notes
   2. Textbook Notes
   3. Handout Notes

Priority #7
❑ Review Test-Review
   Notes to Ace Tests

Priority #8
❑ Write Essays and
   Research Reports
❑ Proofreading Help?

Priority #9
❑ Tutoring Help?

Priority #10
❑ Backup Computer

Priority #11
❑ Pack Book Bag

Priority #12
❑ Socialize with
   Family & Friends
   Time: 8-9 p.m.

Priority #13
❑ Stick to a Regular
   Bedtime: 9-11 p.m.

My Daily Self-Care Journal

1. Practice Gratitude:
I am grateful for...

----

2. Practice Positive Self-Talk:
I am ...

----

3. Practice Meditation:
Close your eyes for 1-5 minutes, and pay attention to your breathing.
Focus your mind on your breathing to become centered and calmer.

----

4. My Healthy Food Energy Choices:

Breakfast Energy: ____

Lunch Energy: ____

Dinner Energy: ____

Study Snack Energy: ____

Eat Whole Foods of Fresh Fruits and Vegetables. Minimize Processed Food and Junk Food.

----

5. My Budget: Save, Spend, and Splurge

Part 1. My Budget

Total Amount of Allowance & Earnings: $ _________ Budget

1. My Savings: Pay Yourself First! $ _________ Savings Bank Account

2. My Pocket Money $ _________ My Wallet

Part 2. My Expenses: Needs & Wants

1. Spend (My Needs): $ _________

2. Splurge (My Wants): $ _________

Total Expenses: $ _________

Part 3.
My Pocket Money Minus My Expenses = $ _________ Balance

6. My After-School Activity:

____

7. My Family Chores:

    1.

    2.

    3.

____

8. A Random Act of Kindness:
    I made a difference in someone else's life by...

____

9. Self-Reflection

❑ Great Day   ❑ Good Day   ❑ Bad Day

1. The Best Part of My Day:

----

2. The Worst Part of My Day:

----

3. How Can I Become a Better Person Tomorrow?

4. Did You Put **LOVE** Into Everything?

____

5. What Is the Stress Level at Home? _______ (#1-10)

6. What Is the Stress Level at School? _______ (#1-10)

____

Practice Building
Good Character Traits

1. Courage
2. Responsibility
3. Kindness
4. Optimisim
5. Loyalty
6. Confidence
7. Honesty
8. Compassion
9. Cooperation
10. Open-Minded
11. Keep Your Word
12. Respectful Communication
13. Courtesy
14. Fair Play

10. ENERGIZE

My Regular Bedtime for POPTART ENERGY Is: _______ p.m.

In Class: My Homework Assignments

Today's Date:

1st Assignment
Class/Subject: _______________
Due Date:

Priority# ___
Estimate Time: ___
Actual Time: ___
❑ Test-Review Notes?
❑ Proofreading Help?
❑ Tutoring Help?

2nd Assignment
Class/Subject: _______________
Due Date:

Priority# ___
Estimate Time: ___
Actual Time: ___
❑ Test-Review Notes?
❑ Proofreading Help?
❑ Tutoring Help?

3rd Assignment
Class/Subject: _______________
Due Date:

Priority# ___
Estimate Time: ___
Actual Time: ___
❑ Test-Review Notes?
❑ Proofreading Help?
❑ Tutoring Help?

4th Assignment
Class/Subject: _______________
Due Date:

Priority# ___
Estimate Time: ___
Actual Time: ___
❑ Test-Review Notes?
❑ Proofreading Help?
❑ Tutoring Help?

5th Assignment
Class/Subject: _______________
Due Date:

Priority# ___
Estimate Time: ___
Actual Time: ___
❑ Test-Review Notes?
❑ Proofreading Help?
❑ Tutoring Help?

6th Assignment
Class/Subject: _______________
Due Date:

Priority# ___
Estimate Time: ___
Actual Time: ___
❑ Test-Review Notes?
❑ Proofreading Help?
❑ Tutoring Help?

At Home: My Study Schedule

7 Shift Study Schedule
45-Minute Study Periods and 15-Minute Breaks

Study Period 1
3-3:45   Subject: __________
15 Minute Study Break (stretch)

Study Period 2
4-4:45   Subject: __________
15 Minute Study Break (stretch)

Study Period 3
5-5:45   Subject:__________
15 Minute Study Break (stretch)

Study Period 4
6-6:45   Subject:__________
15 Minute Study Break (stretch)

Study Period 5
7-7:45   Subject:__________
15 Minute Study Break (stretch)

Study Period 6
8-8:45   Subject:__________
15 Minute Study Break (stretch)

Study Period 7
9-9:45   Subject: __________
15 Minutes: Pack Book Bag for Tomorrow

Regular Bedtime for Energy to Learn

Get Ready for Tomorrow!

❑ 1. Pack Book Bag
❑ 2. Check: Keys, School I.D., Wallet, Money, Pens and Pencils, Assignments
❑ 3. Check Weather (Umbrella? Snow Boots? Sunscreen?)
❑ 4. Q. What Will You Eat for Breakfast and Lunch Tomorrow?
❑ 5. Q. What Will You Wear to School Tomorrow?
❑ 6. Charge Electronic Devices (Computer, Cell Phone, and Watch)
❑ 7. Express Gratitude to Loved Ones (Hugs & Kisses, Love Note, Gift)
❑ 8. Brush & Floss Teeth
❑ 9. Set Alarm Clock

Set Priorities:

Priority #1
❑ Prepare EZ Study Snacks
e.g., Apple Slices, Banana,
Celery & Carrot Sticks

Priority #2
Q. What Time Is Dinner?

Priority #3
❑ Study Period #1
Study for Test!

Priority #4
❑ Study Period #2
What's Due Tomorrow?

Priority #5
❑ What's Due Next Week?

Priority #6
❑ Write Test-Review Notes
to Ace Tests:
1. Class Notes
2. Textbook Notes
3. Handout Notes

Priority #7
❑ Review Test-Review
Notes to Ace Tests

Priority #8
❑ Write Essays and
Research Reports
❑ Proofreading Help?

Priority #9
❑ Tutoring Help?

Priority #10
❑ Backup Computer

Priority #11
❑ Pack Book Bag

Priority #12
❑ Socialize with
Family & Friends
Time: 8-9 p.m.

Priority #13
❑ Stick to a Regular
Bedtime: 9-11 p.m.

My Daily Self-Care Journal

1. **Practice Gratitude:**
   I am grateful for...
----

2. **Practice Positive Self-Talk:**
   I am ...
----

3. **Practice Meditation:**
   Close your eyes for 1-5 minutes, and pay attention to your breathing.
   Focus your mind on your breathing to become centered and calmer.
----

4. **My Healthy Food Energy Choices:**

   Breakfast Energy: ____

   Lunch Energy: ____

   Dinner Energy: ____

   Study Snack Energy: _______________________________________

   Eat Whole Foods of Fresh Fruits and Vegetables. Minimize Processed Food and Junk Food.
----

5. My Budget: Save, Spend, and Splurge

Part 1. My Budget

Total Amount of Allowance & Earnings:　　　　$ ________ Budget

1. My Savings: Pay Yourself First!　　　　$ ________ Savings Bank Account

2. My Pocket Money　　　　$ ________ My Wallet

Part 2. My Expenses: Needs & Wants

1. Spend (My Needs):　　　　$ ________

2. Splurge (My Wants):　　　　$ ________

Total Expenses:　　　　$ ________

Part 3.
My Pocket Money Minus My Expenses =　　　　$ ________ Balance

6. My After-School Activity:

____

7. My Family Chores:

1.

2.

3.

____

8. A Random Act of Kindness:
I made a difference in someone else's life by...

____

9. Self-Reflection

❏ Great Day   ❏ Good Day   ❏ Bad Day

1. The Best Part of My Day:

----

2. The Worst Part of My Day:

----

3. How Can I Become a Better Person Tomorrow?

4. Did You Put **LOVE** Into Everything?

____

5. What Is the Stress Level at Home? ________ (#1-10)

6. What Is the Stress Level at School? ________ (#1-10)

____

Practice Building
Good Character Traits

1. Courage
2. Responsibility
3. Kindness
4. Optimisim
5. Loyalty
6. Confidence
7. Honesty
8. Compassion
9. Cooperation
10. Open-Minded
11. Keep Your Word
12. Respectful Communication
13. Courtesy
14. Fair Play

10. ENERGIZE

My Regular Bedtime for POPTART ENERGY Is: ______ p.m.

In Class: My Homework Assignments

Today's Date:

1st Assignment
Class/Subject: ______________
Due Date:

Priority# ___
Estimate Time: ___
Actual Time: ___
❏ Test-Review Notes?
❏ Proofreading Help?
❏ Tutoring Help?

2nd Assignment
Class/Subject: ______________
Due Date:

Priority# ___
Estimate Time: ___
Actual Time: ___
❏ Test-Review Notes?
❏ Proofreading Help?
❏ Tutoring Help?

3rd Assignment
Class/Subject: ______________
Due Date:

Priority# ___
Estimate Time: ___
Actual Time: ___
❏ Test-Review Notes?
❏ Proofreading Help?
❏ Tutoring Help?

4th Assignment
Class/Subject: ______________
Due Date:

Priority# ___
Estimate Time: ___
Actual Time: ___
❏ Test-Review Notes?
❏ Proofreading Help?
❏ Tutoring Help?

5th Assignment
Class/Subject: ______________
Due Date:

Priority# ___
Estimate Time: ___
Actual Time: ___
❏ Test-Review Notes?
❏ Proofreading Help?
❏ Tutoring Help?

6th Assignment
Class/Subject: ______________
Due Date:

Priority# ___
Estimate Time: ___
Actual Time: ___
❏ Test-Review Notes?
❏ Proofreading Help?
❏ Tutoring Help?

At Home: My Study Schedule

7 Shift Study Schedule
45-Minute Study Periods and 15-Minute Breaks

Study Period 1
3-3:45   Subject: __________
15 Minute Study Break (stretch)

Study Period 2
4-4:45   Subject: __________
15 Minute Study Break (stretch)

Study Period 3
5-5:45   Subject:__________
15 Minute Study Break (stretch)

Study Period 4
6-6:45   Subject:__________
15 Minute Study Break (stretch)

Study Period 5
7-7:45   Subject:__________
15 Minute Study Break (stretch)

Study Period 6
8-8:45   Subject:__________
15 Minute Study Break (stretch)

Study Period 7
9-9:45   Subject: __________
15 Minutes: Pack Book Bag for Tomorrow

Regular Bedtime for Energy to Learn

Get Ready for Tomorrow!

❑ 1. Pack Book Bag
❑ 2. Check: Keys, School I.D., Wallet, Money, Pens and Pencils, Assignments
❑ 3. Check Weather (Umbrella? Snow Boots? Sunscreen?)
❑ 4. Q. What Will You Eat for Breakfast and Lunch Tomorrow?
❑ 5. Q. What Will You Wear to School Tomorrow?
❑ 6. Charge Electronic Devices (Computer, Cell Phone, and Watch)
❑ 7. Express Gratitude to Loved Ones (Hugs & Kisses, Love Note, Gift)
❑ 8. Brush & Floss Teeth
❑ 9. Set Alarm Clock

Set Priorities:

Priority #1
❑ Prepare EZ Study Snacks
  e.g., Apple Slices, Banana,
  Celery & Carrot Sticks

Priority #2
Q. What Time Is Dinner?

Priority #3
❑ Study Period #1
  Study for Test!

Priority #4
❑ Study Period #2
  What's Due Tomorrow?

Priority #5
❑ What's Due Next Week?

Priority #6
❑ Write Test-Review Notes
  to Ace Tests:
  1. Class Notes
  2. Textbook Notes
  3. Handout Notes

Priority #7
❑ Review Test-Review
  Notes to Ace Tests

Priority #8
❑ Write Essays and
  Research Reports
❑ Proofreading Help?

Priority #9
❑ Tutoring Help?

Priority #10
❑ Backup Computer

Priority #11
❑ Pack Book Bag

Priority #12
❑ Socialize with
  Family & Friends
  Time: 8-9 p.m.

Priority #13
❑ Stick to a Regular
  Bedtime: 9-11 p.m.

My Daily Self-Care Journal

1. Practice Gratitude:
   I am grateful for...

----

2. Practice Positive Self-Talk:
   I am ...

----

3. Practice Meditation:
   Close your eyes for 1-5 minutes, and pay attention to your breathing.
   Focus your mind on your breathing to become centered and calmer.

----

4. My Healthy Food Energy Choices:

   Breakfast Energy: ____

   Lunch Energy: ____

   Dinner Energy: ____

   Study Snack Energy: ____

   Eat Whole Foods of Fresh Fruits and Vegetables. Minimize Processed Food and Junk Food.

----

5. My Budget: Save, Spend, and Splurge

Part 1. My Budget

Total Amount of Allowance & Earnings: $ ________ Budget

1. My Savings: Pay Yourself First! $ ________ Savings Bank Account

2. My Pocket Money $ ________ My Wallet

Part 2. My Expenses: Needs & Wants

1. Spend (My Needs): $ ________

2. Splurge (My Wants): $ ________

Total Expenses: $ ________

Part 3.
My Pocket Money Minus My Expenses = $ ________ Balance

6. My After-School Activity:

____

7. My Family Chores:

1.

2.

3.

____

8. A Random Act of Kindness:
I made a difference in someone else's life by...

____

9. Self-Reflection

❑ Great Day   ❑ Good Day   ❑ Bad Day

1. The Best Part of My Day:

----

2. The Worst Part of My Day:

----

3. How Can I Become a Better Person Tomorrow?

4. Did You Put **LOVE** Into Everything?

____

5. What Is the Stress Level at Home? _______ (#1-10)

6. What Is the Stress Level at School? _______ (#1-10)

____

Practice Building
Good Character Traits

1. Courage
2. Responsibility
3. Kindness
4. Optimisim
5. Loyalty
6. Confidence
7. Honesty
8. Compassion
9. Cooperation
10. Open-Minded
11. Keep Your Word
12. Respectful Communication
13. Courtesy
14. Fair Play

10. ENERGIZE

My Regular Bedtime for POPTART ENERGY Is: _______ p.m.

In Class: My Homework Assignments

Today's Date:

1st Assignment
Class/Subject: _____________
Due Date:

Priority# ___
Estimate Time: ___
Actual Time: ___
❑ Test-Review Notes?
❑ Proofreading Help?
❑ Tutoring Help?

2nd Assignment
Class/Subject: _____________
Due Date:

Priority# ___
Estimate Time: ___
Actual Time: ___
❑ Test-Review Notes?
❑ Proofreading Help?
❑ Tutoring Help?

3rd Assignment
Class/Subject: _____________
Due Date:

Priority# ___
Estimate Time: ___
Actual Time: ___
❑ Test-Review Notes?
❑ Proofreading Help?
❑ Tutoring Help?

4th Assignment
Class/Subject: _____________
Due Date:

Priority# ___
Estimate Time: ___
Actual Time: ___
❑ Test-Review Notes?
❑ Proofreading Help?
❑ Tutoring Help?

5th Assignment
Class/Subject: _____________
Due Date:

Priority# ___
Estimate Time: ___
Actual Time: ___
❑ Test-Review Notes?
❑ Proofreading Help?
❑ Tutoring Help?

6th Assignment
Class/Subject: _____________
Due Date:

Priority# ___
Estimate Time: ___
Actual Time: ___
❑ Test-Review Notes?
❑ Proofreading Help?
❑ Tutoring Help?

At Home: My Study Schedule

7 Shift Study Schedule
45-Minute Study Periods and 15-Minute Breaks

Study Period 1
3-3:45   Subject: ___________
15 Minute Study Break (stretch)

Study Period 2
4-4:45   Subject: ___________
15 Minute Study Break (stretch)

Study Period 3
5-5:45   Subject:___________
15 Minute Study Break (stretch)

Study Period 4
6-6:45   Subject:___________
15 Minute Study Break (stretch)

Study Period 5
7-7:45   Subject:___________
15 Minute Study Break (stretch)

Study Period 6
8-8:45   Subject:___________
15 Minute Study Break (stretch)

Study Period 7
9-9:45   Subject: ___________
15 Minutes: Pack Book Bag for Tomorrow

Regular Bedtime for Energy to Learn

Get Ready for Tomorrow!

- ❏ 1. Pack Book Bag
- ❏ 2. Check: Keys, School I.D., Wallet, Money, Pens and Pencils, Assignments
- ❏ 3. Check Weather (Umbrella? Snow Boots? Sunscreen?)
- ❏ 4. Q. What Will You Eat for Breakfast and Lunch Tomorrow?
- ❏ 5. Q. What Will You Wear to School Tomorrow?
- ❏ 6. Charge Electronic Devices (Computer, Cell Phone, and Watch)
- ❏ 7. Express Gratitude to Loved Ones (Hugs & Kisses, Love Note, Gift)
- ❏ 8. Brush & Floss Teeth
- ❏ 9. Set Alarm Clock

Set Priorities:

Priority #1
❏ Prepare EZ Study Snacks
  e.g., Apple Slices, Banana,
  Celery & Carrot Sticks

Priority #2
Q. What Time Is Dinner?

Priority #3
❏ Study Period #1
  Study for Test!

Priority #4
❏ Study Period #2
  What's Due Tomorrow?

Priority #5
❏ What's Due Next Week?

Priority #6
❏ Write Test-Review Notes
  to Ace Tests:
  1. Class Notes
  2. Textbook Notes
  3. Handout Notes

Priority #7
❏ Review Test-Review
  Notes to Ace Tests

Priority #8
❏ Write Essays and
  Research Reports
❏ Proofreading Help?

Priority #9
❏ Tutoring Help?

Priority #10
❏ Backup Computer

Priority #11
❏ Pack Book Bag

Priority #12
❏ Socialize with
  Family & Friends
  Time: 8-9 p.m.

Priority #13
❏ Stick to a Regular
  Bedtime: 9-11 p.m.

My Daily Self-Care Journal

1. **Practice Gratitude:**
   I am grateful for...
----
2. **Practice Positive Self-Talk:**
   I am ...
----
3. **Practice Meditation:**
   Close your eyes for 1-5 minutes, and pay attention to your breathing.
   Focus your mind on your breathing to become centered and calmer.
----
4. **My Healthy Food Energy Choices:**

   Breakfast Energy: ____

   Lunch Energy: ____

   Dinner Energy: ____

   Study Snack Energy: ______________________________________

   Eat Whole Foods of Fresh Fruits and Vegetables. Minimize Processed Food and Junk Food.
----

5. My Budget: Save, Spend, and Splurge

Part 1. My Budget

Total Amount of Allowance & Earnings: $ ________ Budget

1. My Savings: Pay Yourself First! $ ________ Savings Bank Account

2. My Pocket Money $ ________ My Wallet

Part 2. My Expenses: Needs & Wants

1. Spend (My Needs): $ ________

2. Splurge (My Wants): $ ________

Total Expenses: $ ________

Part 3.
My Pocket Money Minus My Expenses = $ ________ Balance

6. My After-School Activity:

____

7. My Family Chores:

    1.

    2.

    3.

____

8. A Random Act of Kindness:
   I made a difference in someone else's life by...

____

9. Self-Reflection

❏ Great Day   ❏ Good Day   ❏ Bad Day

1. The Best Part of My Day:

----

2. The Worst Part of My Day:

----

3. How Can I Become a Better Person Tomorrow?

4. Did You Put **LOVE** Into Everything?

____

5. What Is the Stress Level at Home? _______ (#1-10)

6. What Is the Stress Level at School? _______ (#1-10)

____

Practice Building
Good Character Traits

1. Courage
2. Responsibility
3. Kindness
4. Optimisim
5. Loyalty
6. Confidence
7. Honesty
8. Compassion
9. Cooperation
10. Open-Minded
11. Keep Your Word
12. Respectful Communication
13. Courtesy
14. Fair Play

10. ENERGIZE

My Regular Bedtime for POPTART ENERGY Is: _______ p.m.

In Class: My Homework Assignments

Today's Date:

1st Assignment
Class/Subject: _______________
Due Date:

Priority# ___
Estimate Time: ___
Actual Time: ___
❏ Test-Review Notes?
❏ Proofreading Help?
❏ Tutoring Help?

2nd Assignment
Class/Subject: _______________
Due Date:

Priority# ___
Estimate Time: ___
Actual Time: ___
❏ Test-Review Notes?
❏ Proofreading Help?
❏ Tutoring Help?

3rd Assignment
Class/Subject: _______________
Due Date:

Priority# ___
Estimate Time: ___
Actual Time: ___
❏ Test-Review Notes?
❏ Proofreading Help?
❏ Tutoring Help?

4th Assignment
Class/Subject: _______________
Due Date:

Priority# ___
Estimate Time: ___
Actual Time: ___
❏ Test-Review Notes?
❏ Proofreading Help?
❏ Tutoring Help?

5th Assignment
Class/Subject: _______________
Due Date:

Priority# ___
Estimate Time: ___
Actual Time: ___
❏ Test-Review Notes?
❏ Proofreading Help?
❏ Tutoring Help?

6th Assignment
Class/Subject: _______________
Due Date:

Priority# ___
Estimate Time: ___
Actual Time: ___
❏ Test-Review Notes?
❏ Proofreading Help?
❏ Tutoring Help?

At Home: My Study Schedule

7 Shift Study Schedule
45-Minute Study Periods and 15-Minute Breaks

Study Period 1
3-3:45   Subject: __________
15 Minute Study Break (stretch)

Study Period 2
4-4:45   Subject: __________
15 Minute Study Break (stretch)

Study Period 3
5-5:45   Subject:__________
15 Minute Study Break (stretch)

Study Period 4
6-6:45   Subject:__________
15 Minute Study Break (stretch)

Study Period 5
7-7:45   Subject:__________
15 Minute Study Break (stretch)

Study Period 6
8-8:45   Subject:__________
15 Minute Study Break (stretch)

Study Period 7
9-9:45   Subject: __________
15 Minutes: Pack Book Bag for Tomorrow

Regular Bedtime for Energy to Learn

Get Ready for Tomorrow!

❑ 1. Pack Book Bag
❑ 2. Check: Keys, School I.D., Wallet, Money, Pens and Pencils, Assignments
❑ 3. Check Weather (Umbrella? Snow Boots? Sunscreen?)
❑ 4. Q. What Will You Eat for Breakfast and Lunch Tomorrow?
❑ 5. Q. What Will You Wear to School Tomorrow?
❑ 6. Charge Electronic Devices (Computer, Cell Phone, and Watch)
❑ 7. Express Gratitude to Loved Ones (Hugs & Kisses, Love Note, Gift)
❑ 8. Brush & Floss Teeth
❑ 9. Set Alarm Clock

Set Priorities:

Priority #1
❑ Prepare EZ Study Snacks
   e.g., Apple Slices, Banana,
   Celery & Carrot Sticks

Priority #2
Q. What Time Is Dinner?

Priority #3
❑ Study Period #1
   Study for Test!

Priority #4
❑ Study Period #2
   What's Due Tomorrow?

Priority #5
❑ What's Due Next Week?

Priority #6
❑ Write Test-Review Notes
   to Ace Tests:
   1. Class Notes
   2. Textbook Notes
   3. Handout Notes

Priority #7
❑ Review Test-Review
   Notes to Ace Tests

Priority #8
❑ Write Essays and
   Research Reports
❑ Proofreading Help?

Priority #9
❑ Tutoring Help?

Priority #10
❑ Backup Computer

Priority #11
❑ Pack Book Bag

Priority #12
❑ Socialize with
   Family & Friends
   Time: 8-9 p.m.

Priority #13
❑ Stick to a Regular
   Bedtime: 9-11 p.m.

My Daily Self-Care Journal

1. Practice Gratitude:
I am grateful for...

----

2. Practice Positive Self-Talk:
I am ...

----

3. Practice Meditation:
Close your eyes for 1-5 minutes, and pay attention to your breathing.
Focus your mind on your breathing to become centered and calmer.

----

4. My Healthy Food Energy Choices:

Breakfast Energy: ____

Lunch Energy: ____

Dinner Energy: ____

Study Snack Energy: ____

Eat Whole Foods of Fresh Fruits and Vegetables. Minimize Processed Food and Junk Food.

----

5. My Budget: Save, Spend, and Splurge

Part 1. My Budget

Total Amount of Allowance & Earnings: $ ________ Budget

1. My Savings: Pay Yourself First! $ ________ Savings Bank Account

2. My Pocket Money $ ________ My Wallet

Part 2. My Expenses: Needs & Wants

1. Spend (My Needs): $ ________

2. Splurge (My Wants): $ ________

Total Expenses: $ ________

Part 3.
My Pocket Money Minus My Expenses = $ ________ Balance

6. My After-School Activity:

____

7. My Family Chores:

   1.

   2.

   3.

____

8. A Random Act of Kindness:
   I made a difference in someone else's life by...

____

9. Self-Reflection

❑ Great Day   ❑ Good Day   ❑ Bad Day

1. The Best Part of My Day:

----

2. The Worst Part of My Day:

----

3. How Can I Become a Better Person Tomorrow?

4. Did You Put **LOVE** Into Everything?

----

5. What Is the Stress Level at Home? ________ (#1-10)

6. What Is the Stress Level at School? ________ (#1-10)

Practice Building
Good Character Traits

1. Courage
2. Responsibility
3. Kindness
4. Optimisim
5. Loyalty
6. Confidence
7. Honesty
8. Compassion
9. Cooperation
10. Open-Minded
11. Keep Your Word
12. Respectful Communication
13. Courtesy
14. Fair Play

10. ENERGIZE

My Regular Bedtime for POPTART ENERGY Is: ______ p.m.

In Class: My Homework Assignments

Today's Date:

1st Assignment
Class/Subject: _______________
Due Date:

Priority# ___
Estimate Time: ___
Actual Time: ___
❏ Test-Review Notes?
❏ Proofreading Help?
❏ Tutoring Help?

2nd Assignment
Class/Subject: _______________
Due Date:

Priority# ___
Estimate Time: ___
Actual Time: ___
❏ Test-Review Notes?
❏ Proofreading Help?
❏ Tutoring Help?

3rd Assignment
Class/Subject: _______________
Due Date:

Priority# ___
Estimate Time: ___
Actual Time: ___
❏ Test-Review Notes?
❏ Proofreading Help?
❏ Tutoring Help?

4th Assignment
Class/Subject: _______________
Due Date:

Priority# ___
Estimate Time: ___
Actual Time: ___
❏ Test-Review Notes?
❏ Proofreading Help?
❏ Tutoring Help?

5th Assignment
Class/Subject: _______________
Due Date:

Priority# ___
Estimate Time: ___
Actual Time: ___
❏ Test-Review Notes?
❏ Proofreading Help?
❏ Tutoring Help?

6th Assignment
Class/Subject: _______________
Due Date:

Priority# ___
Estimate Time: ___
Actual Time: ___
❏ Test-Review Notes?
❏ Proofreading Help?
❏ Tutoring Help?

At Home: My Study Schedule

7 Shift Study Schedule
45-Minute Study Periods and 15-Minute Breaks

Study Period 1
3-3:45   Subject: __________
15 Minute Study Break (stretch)

Study Period 2
4-4:45   Subject: __________
15 Minute Study Break (stretch)

Study Period 3
5-5:45   Subject:__________
15 Minute Study Break (stretch)

Study Period 4
6-6:45   Subject:__________
15 Minute Study Break (stretch)

Study Period 5
7-7:45   Subject:__________
15 Minute Study Break (stretch)

Study Period 6
8-8:45   Subject:__________
15 Minute Study Break (stretch)

Study Period 7
9-9:45   Subject: __________
15 Minutes: Pack Book Bag for Tomorrow

Regular Bedtime for Energy to Learn

Get Ready for Tomorrow!

❑ 1. Pack Book Bag
❑ 2. Check: Keys, School I.D., Wallet, Money, Pens and Pencils, Assignments
❑ 3. Check Weather (Umbrella? Snow Boots? Sunscreen?)
❑ 4. Q. What Will You Eat for Breakfast and Lunch Tomorrow?
❑ 5. Q. What Will You Wear to School Tomorrow?
❑ 6. Charge Electronic Devices (Computer, Cell Phone, and Watch)
❑ 7. Express Gratitude to Loved Ones (Hugs & Kisses, Love Note, Gift)
❑ 8. Brush & Floss Teeth
❑ 9. Set Alarm Clock

Set Priorities:

Priority #1
❑ Prepare EZ Study Snacks
e.g., Apple Slices, Banana,
Celery & Carrot Sticks

Priority #2
Q. What Time Is Dinner?

Priority #3
❑ Study Period #1
Study for Test!

Priority #4
❑ Study Period #2
What's Due Tomorrow?

Priority #5
❑ What's Due Next Week?

Priority #6
❑ Write Test-Review Notes
to Ace Tests:
1. Class Notes
2. Textbook Notes
3. Handout Notes

Priority #7
❑ Review Test-Review
Notes to Ace Tests

Priority #8
❑ Write Essays and
Research Reports
❑ Proofreading Help?

Priority #9
❑ Tutoring Help?

Priority #10
❑ Backup Computer

Priority #11
❑ Pack Book Bag

Priority #12
❑ Socialize with
Family & Friends
Time: 8-9 p.m.

Priority #13
❑ Stick to a Regular
Bedtime: 9-11 p.m.

My Daily Self-Care Journal

1. **Practice Gratitude:**
   I am grateful for...

---

2. **Practice Positive Self-Talk:**
   I am ...

---

3. **Practice Meditation:**
   Close your eyes for 1-5 minutes, and pay attention to your breathing.
   Focus your mind on your breathing to become centered and calmer.

---

4. **My Healthy Food Energy Choices:**

   Breakfast Energy: ____

   Lunch Energy: ____

   Dinner Energy: ____

   Study Snack Energy: ____

   Eat Whole Foods of Fresh Fruits and Vegetables. Minimize Processed Food and Junk Food.

---

5. My Budget: Save, Spend, and Splurge

Part 1. My Budget

Total Amount of Allowance & Earnings: $ _________ Budget

1. My Savings: Pay Yourself First! $ _________ Savings Bank Account

2. My Pocket Money $ _________ My Wallet

Part 2. My Expenses: Needs & Wants

1. Spend (My Needs): $ _________

2. Splurge (My Wants): $ _________

Total Expenses: $ _________

Part 3.
My Pocket Money Minus My Expenses = $ _________ Balance

6. My After-School Activity:

____

7. My Family Chores:

1.

2.

3.

____

8. A Random Act of Kindness:
I made a difference in someone else's life by...

____

9. Self-Reflection

❑ Great Day   ❑ Good Day   ❑ Bad Day

1. The Best Part of My Day:

----

2. The Worst Part of My Day:

----

3. How Can I Become a Better Person Tomorrow?

4. Did You Put **LOVE** Into Everything?

____

5. What Is the Stress Level at Home? ________ (#1-10)

6. What Is the Stress Level at School? ________ (#1-10)

____

Practice Building
Good Character Traits

1. Courage
2. Responsibility
3. Kindness
4. Optimisim
5. Loyalty
6. Confidence
7. Honesty
8. Compassion
9. Cooperation
10. Open-Minded
11. Keep Your Word
12. Respectful Communication
13. Courtesy
14. Fair Play

10. ENERGIZE

My Regular Bedtime for POPTART ENERGY Is: ______ p.m.

In Class: My Homework Assignments

Today's Date:

1st Assignment
Class/Subject: ______________
Due Date:

Priority# ___
Estimate Time: ___
Actual Time: ___
❑ Test-Review Notes?
❑ Proofreading Help?
❑ Tutoring Help?

2nd Assignment
Class/Subject: ______________
Due Date:

Priority# ___
Estimate Time: ___
Actual Time: ___
❑ Test-Review Notes?
❑ Proofreading Help?
❑ Tutoring Help?

3rd Assignment
Class/Subject: ______________
Due Date:

Priority# ___
Estimate Time: ___
Actual Time: ___
❑ Test-Review Notes?
❑ Proofreading Help?
❑ Tutoring Help?

4th Assignment
Class/Subject: ______________
Due Date:

Priority# ___
Estimate Time: ___
Actual Time: ___
❑ Test-Review Notes?
❑ Proofreading Help?
❑ Tutoring Help?

5th Assignment
Class/Subject: ______________
Due Date:

Priority# ___
Estimate Time: ___
Actual Time: ___
❑ Test-Review Notes?
❑ Proofreading Help?
❑ Tutoring Help?

6th Assignment
Class/Subject: ______________
Due Date:

Priority# ___
Estimate Time: ___
Actual Time: ___
❑ Test-Review Notes?
❑ Proofreading Help?
❑ Tutoring Help?

At Home: My Study Schedule

7 Shift Study Schedule
45-Minute Study Periods and 15-Minute Breaks

Study Period 1
3-3:45   Subject: __________
15 Minute Study Break (stretch)

Study Period 2
4-4:45   Subject: __________
15 Minute Study Break (stretch)

Study Period 3
5-5:45   Subject:__________
15 Minute Study Break (stretch)

Study Period 4
6-6:45   Subject:__________
15 Minute Study Break (stretch)

Study Period 5
7-7:45   Subject:__________
15 Minute Study Break (stretch)

Study Period 6
8-8:45   Subject:__________
15 Minute Study Break (stretch)

Study Period 7
9-9:45   Subject: __________
15 Minutes: Pack Book Bag for Tomorrow

Regular Bedtime for Energy to Learn

Get Ready for Tomorrow!

❑ 1. Pack Book Bag
❑ 2. Check: Keys, School I.D., Wallet, Money, Pens and Pencils, Assignments
❑ 3. Check Weather (Umbrella? Snow Boots? Sunscreen?)
❑ 4. Q. What Will You Eat for Breakfast and Lunch Tomorrow?
❑ 5. Q. What Will You Wear to School Tomorrow?
❑ 6. Charge Electronic Devices (Computer, Cell Phone, and Watch)
❑ 7. Express Gratitude to Loved Ones (Hugs & Kisses, Love Note, Gift)
❑ 8. Brush & Floss Teeth
❑ 9. Set Alarm Clock

Set Priorities:

Priority #1
❑ Prepare EZ Study Snacks
e.g., Apple Slices, Banana,
Celery & Carrot Sticks

Priority #2
Q. What Time Is Dinner?

Priority #3
❑ Study Period #1
Study for Test!

Priority #4
❑ Study Period #2
What's Due Tomorrow?

Priority #5
❑ What's Due Next Week?

Priority #6
❑ Write Test-Review Notes
to Ace Tests:
1. Class Notes
2. Textbook Notes
3. Handout Notes

Priority #7
❑ Review Test-Review
Notes to Ace Tests

Priority #8
❑ Write Essays and
Research Reports
❑ Proofreading Help?

Priority #9
❑ Tutoring Help?

Priority #10
❑ Backup Computer

Priority #11
❑ Pack Book Bag

Priority #12
❑ Socialize with
Family & Friends
Time: 8-9 p.m.

Priority #13
❑ Stick to a Regular
Bedtime: 9-11 p.m.

My Daily Self-Care Journal

1. **Practice Gratitude:**
   I am grateful for...
----

2. **Practice Positive Self-Talk:**
   I am ...
----

3. **Practice Meditation:**
   Close your eyes for 1-5 minutes, and pay attention to your breathing.
   Focus your mind on your breathing to become centered and calmer.
----

4. **My Healthy Food Energy Choices:**

   Breakfast Energy: ____

   Lunch Energy: ____

   Dinner Energy: ____

   Study Snack Energy: ____

   Eat Whole Foods of Fresh Fruits and Vegetables. Minimize Processed Food and Junk Food.
----

5. My Budget: Save, Spend, and Splurge

Part 1. My Budget

Total Amount of Allowance & Earnings: $ ________ Budget

1. My Savings: Pay Yourself First! $ ________ Savings Bank Account

2. My Pocket Money $ ________ My Wallet

Part 2. My Expenses: Needs & Wants

1. Spend (My Needs): $ ________

2. Splurge (My Wants): $ ________

Total Expenses: $ ________

Part 3.
My Pocket Money Minus My Expenses = $ ________ Balance

6. My After-School Activity:

____

7. My Family Chores:

    1.

    2.

    3.

____

8. A Random Act of Kindness:
   I made a difference in someone else's life by...

____

9. Self-Reflection

❏ Great Day   ❏ Good Day   ❏ Bad Day

1. The Best Part of My Day:

- -

2. The Worst Part of My Day:

- -

3. How Can I Become a Better Person Tomorrow?

4. Did You Put **LOVE** Into Everything?

____

5. What Is the Stress Level at Home?   _______ (#1-10)

6. What Is the Stress Level at School?   _______ (#1-10)

____

Practice Building
Good Character Traits

1. Courage
2. Responsibility
3. Kindness
4. Optimisim
5. Loyalty
6. Confidence
7. Honesty
8. Compassion
9. Cooperation
10. Open-Minded
11. Keep Your Word
12. Respectful Communication
13. Courtesy
14. Fair Play

10. ENERGIZE

My Regular Bedtime for POPTART ENERGY Is: _______ p.m.

In Class: My Homework Assignments

Today's Date:

1st Assignment
Class/Subject: _______________
Due Date:

Priority# ___
Estimate Time: ___
Actual Time: ___
❑ Test-Review Notes?
❑ Proofreading Help?
❑ Tutoring Help?

2nd Assignment
Class/Subject: _______________
Due Date:

Priority# ___
Estimate Time: ___
Actual Time: ___
❑ Test-Review Notes?
❑ Proofreading Help?
❑ Tutoring Help?

3rd Assignment
Class/Subject: _______________
Due Date:

Priority# ___
Estimate Time: ___
Actual Time: ___
❑ Test-Review Notes?
❑ Proofreading Help?
❑ Tutoring Help?

4th Assignment
Class/Subject: _______________
Due Date:

Priority# ___
Estimate Time: ___
Actual Time: ___
❑ Test-Review Notes?
❑ Proofreading Help?
❑ Tutoring Help?

5th Assignment
Class/Subject: _______________
Due Date:

Priority# ___
Estimate Time: ___
Actual Time: ___
❑ Test-Review Notes?
❑ Proofreading Help?
❑ Tutoring Help?

6th Assignment
Class/Subject: _______________
Due Date:

Priority# ___
Estimate Time: ___
Actual Time: ___
❑ Test-Review Notes?
❑ Proofreading Help?
❑ Tutoring Help?

At Home: My Study Schedule

7 Shift Study Schedule
45-Minute Study Periods and 15-Minute Breaks

Study Period 1
3-3:45   Subject: __________
15 Minute Study Break (stretch)

Study Period 2
4-4:45   Subject: __________
15 Minute Study Break (stretch)

Study Period 3
5-5:45   Subject:__________
15 Minute Study Break (stretch)

Study Period 4
6-6:45   Subject:__________
15 Minute Study Break (stretch)

Study Period 5
7-7:45   Subject:__________
15 Minute Study Break (stretch)

Study Period 6
8-8:45   Subject:__________
15 Minute Study Break (stretch)

Study Period 7
9-9:45   Subject: __________
15 Minutes: Pack Book Bag for Tomorrow

Regular Bedtime for Energy to Learn

Get Ready for Tomorrow!

❑ 1. Pack Book Bag
❑ 2. Check: Keys, School I.D., Wallet, Money, Pens and Pencils, Assignments
❑ 3. Check Weather (Umbrella? Snow Boots? Sunscreen?)
❑ 4. Q. What Will You Eat for Breakfast and Lunch Tomorrow?
❑ 5. Q. What Will You Wear to School Tomorrow?
❑ 6. Charge Electronic Devices (Computer, Cell Phone, and Watch)
❑ 7. Express Gratitude to Loved Ones (Hugs & Kisses, Love Note, Gift)
❑ 8. Brush & Floss Teeth
❑ 9. Set Alarm Clock

Set Priorities:

Priority #1
❑ Prepare EZ Study Snacks
  e.g., Apple Slices, Banana,
  Celery & Carrot Sticks

Priority #2
Q. What Time Is Dinner?

Priority #3
❑ Study Period #1
  Study for Test!

Priority #4
❑ Study Period #2
  What's Due Tomorrow?

Priority #5
❑ What's Due Next Week?

Priority #6
❑ Write Test-Review Notes
  to Ace Tests:
    1. Class Notes
    2. Textbook Notes
    3. Handout Notes

Priority #7
❑ Review Test-Review
  Notes to Ace Tests

Priority #8
❑ Write Essays and
  Research Reports
❑ Proofreading Help?

Priority #9
❑ Tutoring Help?

Priority #10
❑ Backup Computer

Priority #11
❑ Pack Book Bag

Priority #12
❑ Socialize with
  Family & Friends
  Time: 8-9 p.m.

Priority #13
❑ Stick to a Regular
  Bedtime: 9-11 p.m.

My Daily Self-Care Journal

1. **Practice Gratitude:**
   I am grateful for...
   ----

2. **Practice Positive Self-Talk:**
   I am ...
   ----

3. **Practice Meditation:**
   Close your eyes for 1-5 minutes, and pay attention to your breathing.
   Focus your mind on your breathing to become centered and calmer.
   ----

4. **My Healthy Food Energy Choices:**

   Breakfast Energy: ____

   Lunch Energy: ____

   Dinner Energy: ____

   Study Snack Energy: ____

   Eat Whole Foods of Fresh Fruits and Vegetables. Minimize Processed Food and Junk Food.
   ----

5. My Budget: Save, Spend, and Splurge

Part 1. My Budget

Total Amount of Allowance & Earnings: $ ________ Budget

1. My Savings: Pay Yourself First! $ ________ Savings Bank Account

2. My Pocket Money $ ________ My Wallet

Part 2. My Expenses: Needs & Wants

1. Spend (My Needs): $ ________

2. Splurge (My Wants): $ ________

Total Expenses: $ ________

Part 3.
My Pocket Money Minus My Expenses = $ ________ Balance

6. My After-School Activity:

____

7. My Family Chores:

1.

2.

3.

____

8. A Random Act of Kindness:
   I made a difference in someone else's life by...

____

9. Self-Reflection

❑ Great Day   ❑ Good Day   ❑ Bad Day

1. The Best Part of My Day:

----

2. The Worst Part of My Day:

----

3. How Can I Become a Better Person Tomorrow?

4. Did You Put **LOVE** Into Everything?

____

5. What Is the Stress Level at Home? _______ (#1-10)

6. What Is the Stress Level at School? _______ (#1-10)

____

Practice Building
Good Character Traits

1. Courage
2. Responsibility
3. Kindness
4. Optimisim
5. Loyalty
6. Confidence
7. Honesty
8. Compassion
9. Cooperation
10. Open-Minded
11. Keep Your Word
12. Respectful Communication
13. Courtesy
14. Fair Play

10. ENERGIZE

My Regular Bedtime for POPTART ENERGY Is: _______ p.m.

In Class: My Homework Assignments

Today's Date:

1st Assignment
Class/Subject: _____________
Due Date:

Priority# ___
Estimate Time: ___
Actual Time: ___
❑ Test-Review Notes?
❑ Proofreading Help?
❑ Tutoring Help?

- -

2nd Assignment
Class/Subject: _____________
Due Date:

Priority# ___
Estimate Time: ___
Actual Time: ___
❑ Test-Review Notes?
❑ Proofreading Help?
❑ Tutoring Help?

- -

3rd Assignment
Class/Subject: _____________
Due Date:

Priority# ___
Estimate Time: ___
Actual Time: ___
❑ Test-Review Notes?
❑ Proofreading Help?
❑ Tutoring Help?

- -

4th Assignment
Class/Subject: _____________
Due Date:

Priority# ___
Estimate Time: ___
Actual Time: ___
❑ Test-Review Notes?
❑ Proofreading Help?
❑ Tutoring Help?

- -

5th Assignment
Class/Subject: _____________
Due Date:

Priority# ___
Estimate Time: ___
Actual Time: ___
❑ Test-Review Notes?
❑ Proofreading Help?
❑ Tutoring Help?

- -

6th Assignment
Class/Subject: _____________
Due Date:

Priority# ___
Estimate Time: ___
Actual Time: ___
❑ Test-Review Notes?
❑ Proofreading Help?
❑ Tutoring Help?

At Home: My Study Schedule

7 Shift Study Schedule
45-Minute Study Periods and 15-Minute Breaks

Study Period 1
3-3:45   Subject: __________
15 Minute Study Break (stretch)

Study Period 2
4-4:45   Subject: __________
15 Minute Study Break (stretch)

Study Period 3
5-5:45   Subject:__________
15 Minute Study Break (stretch)

Study Period 4
6-6:45   Subject:__________
15 Minute Study Break (stretch)

Study Period 5
7-7:45   Subject:__________
15 Minute Study Break (stretch)

Study Period 6
8-8:45   Subject:__________
15 Minute Study Break (stretch)

Study Period 7
9-9:45   Subject: __________
15 Minutes: Pack Book Bag for Tomorrow

Regular Bedtime for Energy to Learn

Get Ready for Tomorrow!

❑ 1. Pack Book Bag
❑ 2. Check: Keys, School I.D., Wallet, Money, Pens and Pencils, Assignments
❑ 3. Check Weather (Umbrella? Snow Boots? Sunscreen?)
❑ 4. Q. What Will You Eat for Breakfast and Lunch Tomorrow?
❑ 5. Q. What Will You Wear to School Tomorrow?
❑ 6. Charge Electronic Devices (Computer, Cell Phone, and Watch)
❑ 7. Express Gratitude to Loved Ones (Hugs & Kisses, Love Note, Gift)
❑ 8. Brush & Floss Teeth
❑ 9. Set Alarm Clock

Set Priorities:

Priority #1
❑ Prepare **EZ** Study Snacks
   e.g., Apple Slices, Banana,
   Celery & Carrot Sticks

Priority #2
Q. What Time Is Dinner?

Priority #3
❑ Study Period #1
   Study for Test!

Priority #4
❑ Study Period #2
   What's Due Tomorrow?

Priority #5
❑ What's Due Next Week?

Priority #6
❑ Write Test-Review Notes
   to Ace Tests:
   1. Class Notes
   2. Textbook Notes
   3. Handout Notes

Priority #7
❑ Review Test-Review
   Notes to Ace Tests

Priority #8
❑ Write Essays and
   Research Reports
❑ Proofreading Help?

Priority #9
❑ Tutoring Help?

Priority #10
❑ Backup Computer

Priority #11
❑ Pack Book Bag

Priority #12
❑ Socialize with
   Family & Friends
   Time: 8-9 p.m.

Priority #13
❑ Stick to a Regular
   Bedtime: 9-11 p.m.

My Daily Self-Care Journal

1. Practice Gratitude:
I am grateful for...

----

2. Practice Positive Self-Talk:
I am ...

----

3. Practice Meditation:
Close your eyes for 1-5 minutes, and pay attention to your breathing.
Focus your mind on your breathing to become centered and calmer.

----

4. My Healthy Food Energy Choices:

Breakfast Energy: ____

Lunch Energy: ____

Dinner Energy: ____

Study Snack Energy: ____

Eat Whole Foods of Fresh Fruits and Vegetables. Minimize Processed Food and Junk Food.

----

5. My Budget: Save, Spend, and Splurge

Part 1. My Budget

Total Amount of Allowance & Earnings: $ ________ Budget

1. My Savings: Pay Yourself First! $ ________ Savings Bank Account

2. My Pocket Money $ ________ My Wallet

Part 2. My Expenses: Needs & Wants

1. Spend (My Needs): $ ________

2. Splurge (My Wants): $ ________

Total Expenses: $ ________

Part 3.
My Pocket Money Minus My Expenses = $ ________ Balance

6. My After-School Activity:

____

7. My Family Chores:

1.

2.

3.

____

8. A Random Act of Kindness:
   I made a difference in someone else's life by...

____

9. Self-Reflection

❑ Great Day   ❑ Good Day   ❑ Bad Day

1. The Best Part of My Day:

- -

2. The Worst Part of My Day:

- -

3. How Can I Become a Better Person Tomorrow?

4. Did You Put **LOVE** Into Everything?

____

5. What Is the Stress Level at Home?   _______ (#1-10)

6. What Is the Stress Level at School?   _______ (#1-10)

____

Practice Building
Good Character Traits

1. Courage
2. Responsibility
3. Kindness
4. Optimisim
5. Loyalty
6. Confidence
7. Honesty
8. Compassion
9. Cooperation
10. Open-Minded
11. Keep Your Word
12. Respectful Communication
13. Courtesy
14. Fair Play

10. ENERGIZE

My Regular Bedtime for POPTART ENERGY Is: _______ p.m.

In Class: My Homework Assignments

Today's Date:

1st Assignment
Class/Subject: _______________
Due Date:

Priority# ___
Estimate Time: ___
Actual Time: ___
❑ Test-Review Notes?
❑ Proofreading Help?
❑ Tutoring Help?

2nd Assignment
Class/Subject: _______________
Due Date:

Priority# ___
Estimate Time: ___
Actual Time: ___
❑ Test-Review Notes?
❑ Proofreading Help?
❑ Tutoring Help?

3rd Assignment
Class/Subject: _______________
Due Date:

Priority# ___
Estimate Time: ___
Actual Time: ___
❑ Test-Review Notes?
❑ Proofreading Help?
❑ Tutoring Help?

4th Assignment
Class/Subject: _______________
Due Date:

Priority# ___
Estimate Time: ___
Actual Time: ___
❑ Test-Review Notes?
❑ Proofreading Help?
❑ Tutoring Help?

5th Assignment
Class/Subject: _______________
Due Date:

Priority# ___
Estimate Time: ___
Actual Time: ___
❑ Test-Review Notes?
❑ Proofreading Help?
❑ Tutoring Help?

6th Assignment
Class/Subject: _______________
Due Date:

Priority# ___
Estimate Time: ___
Actual Time: ___
❑ Test-Review Notes?
❑ Proofreading Help?
❑ Tutoring Help?

At Home: My Study Schedule

7 Shift Study Schedule
45-Minute Study Periods and 15-Minute Breaks

Study Period 1
3-3:45   Subject: __________
15 Minute Study Break (stretch)

Study Period 2
4-4:45   Subject: __________
15 Minute Study Break (stretch)

Study Period 3
5-5:45   Subject:__________
15 Minute Study Break (stretch)

Study Period 4
6-6:45   Subject:__________
15 Minute Study Break (stretch)

Study Period 5
7-7:45   Subject:__________
15 Minute Study Break (stretch)

Study Period 6
8-8:45   Subject:__________
15 Minute Study Break (stretch)

Study Period 7
9-9:45   Subject: __________
15 Minutes: Pack Book Bag for Tomorrow

Regular Bedtime for Energy to Learn

Get Ready for Tomorrow!

❑ 1. Pack Book Bag
❑ 2. Check: Keys, School I.D., Wallet, Money, Pens and Pencils, Assignments
❑ 3. Check Weather (Umbrella? Snow Boots? Sunscreen?)
❑ 4. Q. What Will You Eat for Breakfast and Lunch Tomorrow?
❑ 5. Q. What Will You Wear to School Tomorrow?
❑ 6. Charge Electronic Devices (Computer, Cell Phone, and Watch)
❑ 7. Express Gratitude to Loved Ones (Hugs & Kisses, Love Note, Gift)
❑ 8. Brush & Floss Teeth
❑ 9. Set Alarm Clock

Set Priorities:

Priority #1
❑ Prepare **EZ** Study Snacks
e.g., Apple Slices, Banana,
Celery & Carrot Sticks

Priority #2
Q. What Time Is Dinner?

Priority #3
❑ Study Period #1
Study for Test!

Priority #4
❑ Study Period #2
What's Due Tomorrow?

Priority #5
❑ What's Due Next Week?

Priority #6
❑ Write Test-Review Notes
to Ace Tests:
1. Class Notes
2. Textbook Notes
3. Handout Notes

Priority #7
❑ Review Test-Review
Notes to Ace Tests

Priority #8
❑ Write Essays and
Research Reports
❑ Proofreading Help?

Priority #9
❑ Tutoring Help?

Priority #10
❑ Backup Computer

Priority #11
❑ Pack Book Bag

Priority #12
❑ Socialize with
Family & Friends
Time: 8-9 p.m.

Priority #13
❑ Stick to a Regular
Bedtime: 9-11 p.m.

My Daily Self-Care Journal

1. Practice Gratitude:

I am grateful for...

----

2. Practice Positive Self-Talk:

I am ...

----

3. Practice Meditation:

Close your eyes for 1-5 minutes, and pay attention to your breathing.
Focus your mind on your breathing to become centered and calmer.

----

4. My Healthy Food Energy Choices:

Breakfast Energy: ____

Lunch Energy: ____

Dinner Energy: ____

Study Snack Energy: ______________________________________

Eat Whole Foods of Fresh Fruits and Vegetables. Minimize Processed Food and Junk Food.

----

5. My Budget: Save, Spend, and Splurge

Part 1. My Budget

Total Amount of Allowance & Earnings: $ _________ Budget

1. My Savings: Pay Yourself First! $ _________ Savings Bank Account

2. My Pocket Money $ _________ My Wallet

Part 2. My Expenses: Needs & Wants

1. Spend (My Needs): $ _______

2. Splurge (My Wants): $ _______

Total Expenses: $ _______

Part 3.
My Pocket Money Minus My Expenses = $ _______ Balance

6. My After-School Activity:

____

7. My Family Chores:

1.

2.

3.

____

8. A Random Act of Kindness:
I made a difference in someone else's life by...

____

9. Self-Reflection

❑ Great Day   ❑ Good Day   ❑ Bad Day

1. The Best Part of My Day:

----

2. The Worst Part of My Day:

----

3. How Can I Become a Better Person Tomorrow?

4. Did You Put **LOVE** Into Everything?

____

5. What Is the Stress Level at Home? _______ (#1-10)

6. What Is the Stress Level at School? _______ (#1-10)

____

Practice Building
Good Character Traits

1. Courage
2. Responsibility
3. Kindness
4. Optimisim
5. Loyalty
6. Confidence
7. Honesty
8. Compassion
9. Cooperation
10. Open-Minded
11. Keep Your Word
12. Respectful Communication
13. Courtesy
14. Fair Play

10. ENERGIZE

My Regular Bedtime for POPTART ENERGY Is: ______ p.m.

In Class: My Homework Assignments

Today's Date:

1st Assignment
Class/Subject: _______________
Due Date:

Priority# ___
Estimate Time: ___
Actual Time: ___
❏ Test-Review Notes?
❏ Proofreading Help?
❏ Tutoring Help?

2nd Assignment
Class/Subject: _______________
Due Date:

Priority# ___
Estimate Time: ___
Actual Time: ___
❏ Test-Review Notes?
❏ Proofreading Help?
❏ Tutoring Help?

3rd Assignment
Class/Subject: _______________
Due Date:

Priority# ___
Estimate Time: ___
Actual Time: ___
❏ Test-Review Notes?
❏ Proofreading Help?
❏ Tutoring Help?

4th Assignment
Class/Subject: _______________
Due Date:

Priority# ___
Estimate Time: ___
Actual Time: ___
❏ Test-Review Notes?
❏ Proofreading Help?
❏ Tutoring Help?

5th Assignment
Class/Subject: _______________
Due Date:

Priority# ___
Estimate Time: ___
Actual Time: ___
❏ Test-Review Notes?
❏ Proofreading Help?
❏ Tutoring Help?

6th Assignment
Class/Subject: _______________
Due Date:

Priority# ___
Estimate Time: ___
Actual Time: ___
❏ Test-Review Notes?
❏ Proofreading Help?
❏ Tutoring Help?

At Home: My Study Schedule

7 Shift Study Schedule
45-Minute Study Periods and 15-Minute Breaks

Study Period 1
3-3:45   Subject: __________
15 Minute Study Break (stretch)

Study Period 2
4-4:45   Subject: __________
15 Minute Study Break (stretch)

Study Period 3
5-5:45   Subject:__________
15 Minute Study Break (stretch)

Study Period 4
6-6:45   Subject:__________
15 Minute Study Break (stretch)

Study Period 5
7-7:45   Subject:__________
15 Minute Study Break (stretch)

Study Period 6
8-8:45   Subject:__________
15 Minute Study Break (stretch)

Study Period 7
9-9:45   Subject: __________
15 Minutes: Pack Book Bag for Tomorrow

Regular Bedtime for Energy to Learn

Get Ready for Tomorrow!

❑ 1. Pack Book Bag
❑ 2. Check: Keys, School I.D., Wallet, Money, Pens and Pencils, Assignments
❑ 3. Check Weather (Umbrella? Snow Boots? Sunscreen?)
❑ 4. Q. What Will You Eat for Breakfast and Lunch Tomorrow?
❑ 5. Q. What Will You Wear to School Tomorrow?
❑ 6. Charge Electronic Devices (Computer, Cell Phone, and Watch)
❑ 7. Express Gratitude to Loved Ones (Hugs & Kisses, Love Note, Gift)
❑ 8. Brush & Floss Teeth
❑ 9. Set Alarm Clock

Set Priorities:

Priority #1
❑ Prepare EZ Study Snacks
   e.g., Apple Slices, Banana,
   Celery & Carrot Sticks

Priority #2
Q. What Time Is Dinner?

Priority #3
❑ Study Period #1
   Study for Test!

Priority #4
❑ Study Period #2
   What's Due Tomorrow?

Priority #5
❑ What's Due Next Week?

Priority #6
❑ Write Test-Review Notes
   to Ace Tests:
   1. Class Notes
   2. Textbook Notes
   3. Handout Notes

Priority #7
❑ Review Test-Review
   Notes to Ace Tests

Priority #8
❑ Write Essays and
   Research Reports
❑ Proofreading Help?

Priority #9
❑ Tutoring Help?

Priority #10
❑ Backup Computer

Priority #11
❑ Pack Book Bag

Priority #12
❑ Socialize with
   Family & Friends
   Time: 8-9 p.m.

Priority #13
❑ Stick to a Regular
   Bedtime: 9-11 p.m.

My Daily Self-Care Journal

1. Practice Gratitude:
I am grateful for...

----

2. Practice Positive Self-Talk:
I am ...

----

3. Practice Meditation:
Close your eyes for 1-5 minutes, and pay attention to your breathing.
Focus your mind on your breathing to become centered and calmer.

----

4. My Healthy Food Energy Choices:

Breakfast Energy: ____

Lunch Energy: ____

Dinner Energy: ____

Study Snack Energy: ____

Eat Whole Foods of Fresh Fruits and Vegetables. Minimize Processed Food and Junk Food.

----

5. My Budget: Save, Spend, and Splurge

Part 1. My Budget

Total Amount of Allowance & Earnings: $ ________ Budget

1. My Savings: Pay Yourself First! $ ________ Savings Bank Account

2. My Pocket Money $ ________ My Wallet

Part 2. My Expenses: Needs & Wants

1. Spend (My Needs): $ ________

2. Splurge (My Wants): $ ________

Total Expenses: $ ________

Part 3.
My Pocket Money Minus My Expenses = $ ________ Balance

6. My After-School Activity:

____

7. My Family Chores:

1.

2.

3.

____

8. A Random Act of Kindness:
I made a difference in someone else's life by...

____

9. Self-Reflection

❑ Great Day   ❑ Good Day   ❑ Bad Day

1. The Best Part of My Day:

----

2. The Worst Part of My Day:

----

3. How Can I Become a Better Person Tomorrow?

4. Did You Put LOVE Into Everything?

----

5. What Is the Stress Level at Home? _______ (#1-10)

6. What Is the Stress Level at School? _______ (#1-10)

Practice Building
Good Character Traits

1. Courage
2. Responsibility
3. Kindness
4. Optimisim
5. Loyalty
6. Confidence
7. Honesty
8. Compassion
9. Cooperation
10. Open-Minded
11. Keep Your Word
12. Respectful Communication
13. Courtesy
14. Fair Play

10. ENERGIZE

My Regular Bedtime for POPTART ENERGY Is: ______ p.m.

In Class: My Homework Assignments

Today's Date:

1st Assignment
Class/Subject: _______________
Due Date:

Priority# ____
Estimate Time: ____
Actual Time: ____
❑ Test-Review Notes?
❑ Proofreading Help?
❑ Tutoring Help?

2nd Assignment
Class/Subject: _______________
Due Date:

Priority# ____
Estimate Time: ____
Actual Time: ____
❑ Test-Review Notes?
❑ Proofreading Help?
❑ Tutoring Help?

3rd Assignment
Class/Subject: _______________
Due Date:

Priority# ____
Estimate Time: ____
Actual Time: ____
❑ Test-Review Notes?
❑ Proofreading Help?
❑ Tutoring Help?

4th Assignment
Class/Subject: _______________
Due Date:

Priority# ____
Estimate Time: ____
Actual Time: ____
❑ Test-Review Notes?
❑ Proofreading Help?
❑ Tutoring Help?

5th Assignment
Class/Subject: _______________
Due Date:

Priority# ____
Estimate Time: ____
Actual Time: ____
❑ Test-Review Notes?
❑ Proofreading Help?
❑ Tutoring Help?

6th Assignment
Class/Subject: _______________
Due Date:

Priority# ____
Estimate Time: ____
Actual Time: ____
❑ Test-Review Notes?
❑ Proofreading Help?
❑ Tutoring Help?

At Home: My Study Schedule

7 Shift Study Schedule
45-Minute Study Periods and 15-Minute Breaks

Study Period 1
3-3:45   Subject: __________
15 Minute Study Break (stretch)

Study Period 2
4-4:45   Subject: __________
15 Minute Study Break (stretch)

Study Period 3
5-5:45   Subject:__________
15 Minute Study Break (stretch)

Study Period 4
6-6:45   Subject:__________
15 Minute Study Break (stretch)

Study Period 5
7-7:45   Subject:__________
15 Minute Study Break (stretch)

Study Period 6
8-8:45   Subject:__________
15 Minute Study Break (stretch)

Study Period 7
9-9:45   Subject: __________
15 Minutes: Pack Book Bag for Tomorrow

Regular Bedtime for Energy to Learn

Get Ready for Tomorrow!

❑ 1. Pack Book Bag
❑ 2. Check: Keys, School I.D., Wallet, Money, Pens and Pencils, Assignments
❑ 3. Check Weather (Umbrella? Snow Boots? Sunscreen?)
❑ 4. Q. What Will You Eat for Breakfast and Lunch Tomorrow?
❑ 5. Q. What Will You Wear to School Tomorrow?
❑ 6. Charge Electronic Devices (Computer, Cell Phone, and Watch)
❑ 7. Express Gratitude to Loved Ones (Hugs & Kisses, Love Note, Gift)
❑ 8. Brush & Floss Teeth
❑ 9. Set Alarm Clock

Set Priorities:

Priority #1
❑ Prepare **EZ** Study Snacks
e.g., Apple Slices, Banana,
Celery & Carrot Sticks

Priority #2
Q. What Time Is Dinner?

Priority #3
❑ Study Period #1
Study for Test!

Priority #4
❑ Study Period #2
What's Due Tomorrow?

Priority #5
❑ What's Due Next Week?

Priority #6
❑ Write Test-Review Notes
to Ace Tests:
1. Class Notes
2. Textbook Notes
3. Handout Notes

Priority #7
❑ Review Test-Review
Notes to Ace Tests

Priority #8
❑ Write Essays and
Research Reports
❑ Proofreading Help?

Priority #9
❑ Tutoring Help?

Priority #10
❑ Backup Computer

Priority #11
❑ Pack Book Bag

Priority #12
❑ Socialize with
Family & Friends
Time: 8-9 p.m.

Priority #13
❑ Stick to a Regular
Bedtime: 9-11 p.m.

My Daily Self-Care Journal

1. Practice Gratitude:
   I am grateful for...
----

2. Practice Positive Self-Talk:
   I am ...
----

3. Practice Meditation:
   Close your eyes for 1-5 minutes, and pay attention to your breathing.
   Focus your mind on your breathing to become centered and calmer.
----

4. My Healthy Food Energy Choices:

   Breakfast Energy: ____

   Lunch Energy: ____

   Dinner Energy: ____

   Study Snack Energy: ______________________________________

   Eat Whole Foods of Fresh Fruits and Vegetables. Minimize Processed Food and Junk Food.
----

5. My Budget: Save, Spend, and Splurge

Part 1. My Budget

Total Amount of Allowance & Earnings: $ ________ Budget

1. My Savings: Pay Yourself First! $ ________ Savings Bank Account

2. My Pocket Money $ ________ My Wallet

Part 2. My Expenses: Needs & Wants

1. Spend (My Needs): $ ________

2. Splurge (My Wants): $ ________

Total Expenses: $ ________

Part 3.
My Pocket Money Minus My Expenses = $ ________ Balance

6. My After-School Activity:

____

7. My Family Chores:

    1.

    2.

    3.

____

8. A Random Act of Kindness:
I made a difference in someone else's life by...

____

9. Self-Reflection

❑ Great Day   ❑ Good Day   ❑ Bad Day

1. The Best Part of My Day:

- -

2. The Worst Part of My Day:

- -

3. How Can I Become a Better Person Tomorrow?

4. Did You Put LOVE Into Everything?

____

5. What Is the Stress Level at Home? _______ (#1-10)

6. What Is the Stress Level at School? _______ (#1-10)

____

Practice Building
Good Character Traits

1. Courage
2. Responsibility
3. Kindness
4. Optimisim
5. Loyalty
6. Confidence
7. Honesty
8. Compassion
9. Cooperation
10. Open-Minded
11. Keep Your Word
12. Respectful Communication
13. Courtesy
14. Fair Play

10. ENERGIZE

My Regular Bedtime for POPTART ENERGY Is: _______ p.m.

In Class: My Homework Assignments

Today's Date:

1st Assignment
Class/Subject: _____________
Due Date:

Priority# ___
Estimate Time: ___
Actual Time: ___
❑ Test-Review Notes?
❑ Proofreading Help?
❑ Tutoring Help?

2nd Assignment
Class/Subject: _____________
Due Date:

Priority# ___
Estimate Time: ___
Actual Time: ___
❑ Test-Review Notes?
❑ Proofreading Help?
❑ Tutoring Help?

3rd Assignment
Class/Subject: _____________
Due Date:

Priority# ___
Estimate Time: ___
Actual Time: ___
❑ Test-Review Notes?
❑ Proofreading Help?
❑ Tutoring Help?

4th Assignment
Class/Subject: _____________
Due Date:

Priority# ___
Estimate Time: ___
Actual Time: ___
❑ Test-Review Notes?
❑ Proofreading Help?
❑ Tutoring Help?

5th Assignment
Class/Subject: _____________
Due Date:

Priority# ___
Estimate Time: ___
Actual Time: ___
❑ Test-Review Notes?
❑ Proofreading Help?
❑ Tutoring Help?

6th Assignment
Class/Subject: _____________
Due Date:

Priority# ___
Estimate Time: ___
Actual Time: ___
❑ Test-Review Notes?
❑ Proofreading Help?
❑ Tutoring Help?

At Home: My Study Schedule

7 Shift Study Schedule
45-Minute Study Periods and 15-Minute Breaks

Study Period 1
3-3:45   Subject: __________
15 Minute Study Break (stretch)

Study Period 2
4-4:45   Subject: __________
15 Minute Study Break (stretch)

Study Period 3
5-5:45   Subject:__________
15 Minute Study Break (stretch)

Study Period 4
6-6:45   Subject:__________
15 Minute Study Break (stretch)

Study Period 5
7-7:45   Subject:__________
15 Minute Study Break (stretch)

Study Period 6
8-8:45   Subject:__________
15 Minute Study Break (stretch)

Study Period 7
9-9:45   Subject: __________
15 Minutes: Pack Book Bag for Tomorrow

Regular Bedtime for Energy to Learn

Get Ready for Tomorrow!

❑ 1. Pack Book Bag
❑ 2. Check: Keys, School I.D., Wallet, Money, Pens and Pencils, Assignments
❑ 3. Check Weather (Umbrella? Snow Boots? Sunscreen?)
❑ 4. Q. What Will You Eat for Breakfast and Lunch Tomorrow?
❑ 5. Q. What Will You Wear to School Tomorrow?
❑ 6. Charge Electronic Devices (Computer, Cell Phone, and Watch)
❑ 7. Express Gratitude to Loved Ones (Hugs & Kisses, Love Note, Gift)
❑ 8. Brush & Floss Teeth
❑ 9. Set Alarm Clock

Set Priorities:

Priority #1
❑ Prepare EZ Study Snacks
e.g., Apple Slices, Banana,
Celery & Carrot Sticks

Priority #2
Q. What Time Is Dinner?

Priority #3
❑ Study Period #1
Study for Test!

Priority #4
❑ Study Period #2
What's Due Tomorrow?

Priority #5
❑ What's Due Next Week?

Priority #6
❑ Write Test-Review Notes
to Ace Tests:
1. Class Notes
2. Textbook Notes
3. Handout Notes

Priority #7
❑ Review Test-Review
Notes to Ace Tests

Priority #8
❑ Write Essays and
Research Reports
❑ Proofreading Help?

Priority #9
❑ Tutoring Help?

Priority #10
❑ Backup Computer

Priority #11
❑ Pack Book Bag

Priority #12
❑ Socialize with
Family & Friends
Time: 8-9 p.m.

Priority #13
❑ Stick to a Regular
Bedtime: 9-11 p.m.

My Daily Self-Care Journal

1. **Practice Gratitude:**
   I am grateful for...
----

2. **Practice Positive Self-Talk:**
   I am ...
----

3. **Practice Meditation:**
   Close your eyes for 1-5 minutes, and pay attention to your breathing.
   Focus your mind on your breathing to become centered and calmer.
----

4. **My Healthy Food Energy Choices:**

   Breakfast Energy: ____

   Lunch Energy: ____

   Dinner Energy: ____

   Study Snack Energy: _____________________________________

   Eat Whole Foods of Fresh Fruits and Vegetables. Minimize Processed Food and Junk Food.
----

5. My Budget: Save, Spend, and Splurge

Part 1. My Budget

Total Amount of Allowance & Earnings: $ ________ Budget

1. My Savings: Pay Yourself First! $ ________ Savings Bank Account

2. My Pocket Money $ ________ My Wallet

Part 2. My Expenses: Needs & Wants

1. Spend (My Needs): $ ________

2. Splurge (My Wants): $ ________

Total Expenses: $ ________

Part 3.
My Pocket Money Minus My Expenses = $ ________ Balance

6. **My After-School Activity:**

____

7. **My Family Chores:**

    1.

    2.

    3.

____

8. **A Random Act of Kindness:**
   I made a difference in someone else's life by...

____

9. Self-Reflection

❑ Great Day   ❑ Good Day   ❑ Bad Day

1. The Best Part of My Day:

----

2. The Worst Part of My Day:

----

3. How Can I Become a Better Person Tomorrow?

4. Did You Put **LOVE** Into Everything?

____

5. What Is the Stress Level at Home? _______ (#1-10)

6. What Is the Stress Level at School? _______ (#1-10)

____

Practice Building
Good Character Traits

1. Courage
2. Responsibility
3. Kindness
4. Optimisim
5. Loyalty
6. Confidence
7. Honesty
8. Compassion
9. Cooperation
10. Open-Minded
11. Keep Your Word
12. Respectful Communication
13. Courtesy
14. Fair Play

10. ENERGIZE

My Regular Bedtime for POPTART ENERGY Is: ______ p.m.

In Class: My Homework Assignments

Today's Date:

1st Assignment
Class/Subject: _______________
Due Date:

Priority# ___
Estimate Time: ___
Actual Time: ___
❏ Test-Review Notes?
❏ Proofreading Help?
❏ Tutoring Help?

2nd Assignment
Class/Subject: _______________
Due Date:

Priority# ___
Estimate Time: ___
Actual Time: ___
❏ Test-Review Notes?
❏ Proofreading Help?
❏ Tutoring Help?

3rd Assignment
Class/Subject: _______________
Due Date:

Priority# ___
Estimate Time: ___
Actual Time: ___
❏ Test-Review Notes?
❏ Proofreading Help?
❏ Tutoring Help?

4th Assignment
Class/Subject: _______________
Due Date:

Priority# ___
Estimate Time: ___
Actual Time: ___
❏ Test-Review Notes?
❏ Proofreading Help?
❏ Tutoring Help?

5th Assignment
Class/Subject: _______________
Due Date:

Priority# ___
Estimate Time: ___
Actual Time: ___
❏ Test-Review Notes?
❏ Proofreading Help?
❏ Tutoring Help?

6th Assignment
Class/Subject: _______________
Due Date:

Priority# ___
Estimate Time: ___
Actual Time: ___
❏ Test-Review Notes?
❏ Proofreading Help?
❏ Tutoring Help?

At Home: My Study Schedule

7 Shift Study Schedule
45-Minute Study Periods and 15-Minute Breaks

Study Period 1
3-3:45   Subject: __________
15 Minute Study Break (stretch)

Study Period 2
4-4:45   Subject: __________
15 Minute Study Break (stretch)

Study Period 3
5-5:45   Subject:__________
15 Minute Study Break (stretch)

Study Period 4
6-6:45   Subject:__________
15 Minute Study Break (stretch)

Study Period 5
7-7:45   Subject:__________
15 Minute Study Break (stretch)

Study Period 6
8-8:45   Subject:__________
15 Minute Study Break (stretch)

Study Period 7
9-9:45   Subject: __________
15 Minutes: Pack Book Bag for Tomorrow

Regular Bedtime for Energy to Learn

Get Ready for Tomorrow!

❑ 1. Pack Book Bag
❑ 2. Check: Keys, School I.D., Wallet, Money, Pens and Pencils, Assignments
❑ 3. Check Weather (Umbrella? Snow Boots? Sunscreen?)
❑ 4. Q. What Will You Eat for Breakfast and Lunch Tomorrow?
❑ 5. Q. What Will You Wear to School Tomorrow?
❑ 6. Charge Electronic Devices (Computer, Cell Phone, and Watch)
❑ 7. Express Gratitude to Loved Ones (Hugs & Kisses, Love Note, Gift)
❑ 8. Brush & Floss Teeth
❑ 9. Set Alarm Clock

Set Priorities:

Priority #1
❑ Prepare EZ Study Snacks
   e.g., Apple Slices, Banana,
   Celery & Carrot Sticks

Priority #2
Q. What Time Is Dinner?

Priority #3
❑ Study Period #1
   Study for Test!

Priority #4
❑ Study Period #2
   What's Due Tomorrow?

Priority #5
❑ What's Due Next Week?

Priority #6
❑ Write Test-Review Notes
   to Ace Tests:
   1. Class Notes
   2. Textbook Notes
   3. Handout Notes

Priority #7
❑ Review Test-Review
   Notes to Ace Tests

Priority #8
❑ Write Essays and
   Research Reports
❑ Proofreading Help?

Priority #9
❑ Tutoring Help?

Priority #10
❑ Backup Computer

Priority #11
❑ Pack Book Bag

Priority #12
❑ Socialize with
   Family & Friends
   Time: 8-9 p.m.

Priority #13
❑ Stick to a Regular
   Bedtime: 9-11 p.m.

My Daily Self-Care Journal

1. **Practice Gratitude:**
   I am grateful for...
   ----

2. **Practice Positive Self-Talk:**
   I am ...
   ----

3. **Practice Meditation:**
   Close your eyes for 1-5 minutes, and pay attention to your breathing.
   Focus your mind on your breathing to become centered and calmer.
   ----

4. **My Healthy Food Energy Choices:**

   Breakfast Energy: ____

   Lunch Energy: ____

   Dinner Energy: ____

   Study Snack Energy: ____

   Eat Whole Foods of Fresh Fruits and Vegetables. Minimize Processed Food and Junk Food.
   ----

5. My Budget: Save, Spend, and Splurge

Part 1. My Budget

Total Amount of Allowance & Earnings: $ ________ Budget

1. My Savings: Pay Yourself First! $ ________ Savings Bank Account

2. My Pocket Money $ ________ My Wallet

Part 2. My Expenses: Needs & Wants

1. Spend (My Needs): $ ________

2. Splurge (My Wants): $ ________

Total Expenses: $ ________

Part 3.
My Pocket Money Minus My Expenses = $ ________ Balance

6. My After-School Activity:

____

7. My Family Chores:

    1.

    2.

    3.

____

8. A Random Act of Kindness:
   I made a difference in someone else's life by...

____

9. Self-Reflection

❑ Great Day   ❑ Good Day   ❑ Bad Day

1. The Best Part of My Day:

- -

2. The Worst Part of My Day:

- -

3. How Can I Become a Better Person Tomorrow?

4. Did You Put **LOVE** Into Everything?

____

5. What Is the Stress Level at Home? _______ (#1-10)

6. What Is the Stress Level at School? _______ (#1-10)

____

Practice Building
Good Character Traits

1. Courage
2. Responsibility
3. Kindness
4. Optimisim
5. Loyalty
6. Confidence
7. Honesty
8. Compassion
9. Cooperation
10. Open-Minded
11. Keep Your Word
12. Respectful Communication
13. Courtesy
14. Fair Play

10. ENERGIZE

My Regular Bedtime for POPTART ENERGY Is: _______ p.m.

In Class: My Homework Assignments

Today's Date:

1st Assignment
Class/Subject: _______________
Due Date:

Priority# ___
Estimate Time: ___
Actual Time: ___
❑ Test-Review Notes?
❑ Proofreading Help?
❑ Tutoring Help?

2nd Assignment
Class/Subject: _______________
Due Date:

Priority# ___
Estimate Time: ___
Actual Time: ___
❑ Test-Review Notes?
❑ Proofreading Help?
❑ Tutoring Help?

3rd Assignment
Class/Subject: _______________
Due Date:

Priority# ___
Estimate Time: ___
Actual Time: ___
❑ Test-Review Notes?
❑ Proofreading Help?
❑ Tutoring Help?

4th Assignment
Class/Subject: _______________
Due Date:

Priority# ___
Estimate Time: ___
Actual Time: ___
❑ Test-Review Notes?
❑ Proofreading Help?
❑ Tutoring Help?

5th Assignment
Class/Subject: _______________
Due Date:

Priority# ___
Estimate Time: ___
Actual Time: ___
❑ Test-Review Notes?
❑ Proofreading Help?
❑ Tutoring Help?

6th Assignment
Class/Subject: _______________
Due Date:

Priority# ___
Estimate Time: ___
Actual Time: ___
❑ Test-Review Notes?
❑ Proofreading Help?
❑ Tutoring Help?

At Home: My Study Schedule

7 Shift Study Schedule
45-Minute Study Periods and 15-Minute Breaks

Study Period 1
3-3:45   Subject: __________
15 Minute Study Break (stretch)

Study Period 2
4-4:45   Subject: __________
15 Minute Study Break (stretch)

Study Period 3
5-5:45   Subject:__________
15 Minute Study Break (stretch)

Study Period 4
6-6:45   Subject:__________
15 Minute Study Break (stretch)

Study Period 5
7-7:45   Subject:__________
15 Minute Study Break (stretch)

Study Period 6
8-8:45   Subject:__________
15 Minute Study Break (stretch)

Study Period 7
9-9:45   Subject: __________
15 Minutes: Pack Book Bag for Tomorrow

Regular Bedtime for Energy to Learn

Get Ready for Tomorrow!

❑ 1. Pack Book Bag
❑ 2. Check: Keys, School I.D., Wallet, Money, Pens and Pencils, Assignments
❑ 3. Check Weather (Umbrella? Snow Boots? Sunscreen?)
❑ 4. Q. What Will You Eat for Breakfast and Lunch Tomorrow?
❑ 5. Q. What Will You Wear to School Tomorrow?
❑ 6. Charge Electronic Devices (Computer, Cell Phone, and Watch)
❑ 7. Express Gratitude to Loved Ones (Hugs & Kisses, Love Note, Gift)
❑ 8. Brush & Floss Teeth
❑ 9. Set Alarm Clock

Set Priorities:

Priority #1
❑ Prepare EZ Study Snacks
   e.g., Apple Slices, Banana,
   Celery & Carrot Sticks

Priority #2
Q. What Time Is Dinner?

Priority #3
❑ Study Period #1
   Study for Test!

Priority #4
❑ Study Period #2
   What's Due Tomorrow?

Priority #5
❑ What's Due Next Week?

Priority #6
❑ Write Test-Review Notes
   to Ace Tests:
   1. Class Notes
   2. Textbook Notes
   3. Handout Notes

Priority #7
❑ Review Test-Review
   Notes to Ace Tests

Priority #8
❑ Write Essays and
   Research Reports
❑ Proofreading Help?

Priority #9
❑ Tutoring Help?

Priority #10
❑ Backup Computer

Priority #11
❑ Pack Book Bag

Priority #12
❑ Socialize with
   Family & Friends
   Time: 8-9 p.m.

Priority #13
❑ Stick to a Regular
   Bedtime: 9-11 p.m.

My Daily Self-Care Journal

1. Practice Gratitude:

   I am grateful for...

----

2. Practice Positive Self-Talk:

   I am ...

----

3. Practice Meditation:
   Close your eyes for 1-5 minutes, and pay attention to your breathing.
   Focus your mind on your breathing to become centered and calmer.

----

4. My Healthy Food Energy Choices:

   Breakfast Energy: ___________________________________

   Lunch Energy: ___________________________________

   Dinner Energy: ___________________________________

   Study Snack Energy: ___________________________________

   Eat Whole Foods of Fresh Fruits and Vegetables. Minimize Processed Food and Junk Food.

----

5. My Budget: Save, Spend, and Splurge

Part 1. My Budget

Total Amount of Allowance & Earnings: $ ________ Budget

1. My Savings: Pay Yourself First! $ ________ Savings Bank Account

2. My Pocket Money $ ________ My Wallet

Part 2. My Expenses: Needs & Wants

1. Spend (My Needs): $ ________

2. Splurge (My Wants): $ ________

Total Expenses: $ ________

Part 3.
My Pocket Money Minus My Expenses = $ ________ Balance

6. My After-School Activity:

____

7. My Family Chores:

1.

2.

3.

____

8. A Random Act of Kindness:
I made a difference in someone else's life by...

____

9. Self-Reflection

❑ Great Day   ❑ Good Day   ❑ Bad Day

1. The Best Part of My Day:

----

2. The Worst Part of My Day:

----

3. How Can I Become a Better Person Tomorrow?

4. Did You Put **LOVE** Into Everything?

____

5. What Is the Stress Level at Home? _______ (#1-10)

6. What Is the Stress Level at School? _______ (#1-10)

____

Practice Building
Good Character Traits

1. Courage
2. Responsibility
3. Kindness
4. Optimisim
5. Loyalty
6. Confidence
7. Honesty
8. Compassion
9. Cooperation
10. Open-Minded
11. Keep Your Word
12. Respectful Communication
13. Courtesy
14. Fair Play

10. ENERGIZE

My Regular Bedtime for POPTART ENERGY Is: _______ p.m.

In Class: My Homework Assignments

Today's Date:

1st Assignment
Class/Subject: ______________
Due Date:

Priority# ___
Estimate Time: ___
Actual Time: ___
❑ Test-Review Notes?
❑ Proofreading Help?
❑ Tutoring Help?

2nd Assignment
Class/Subject: ______________
Due Date:

Priority# ___
Estimate Time: ___
Actual Time: ___
❑ Test-Review Notes?
❑ Proofreading Help?
❑ Tutoring Help?

3rd Assignment
Class/Subject: ______________
Due Date:

Priority# ___
Estimate Time: ___
Actual Time: ___
❑ Test-Review Notes?
❑ Proofreading Help?
❑ Tutoring Help?

4th Assignment
Class/Subject: ______________
Due Date:

Priority# ___
Estimate Time: ___
Actual Time: ___
❑ Test-Review Notes?
❑ Proofreading Help?
❑ Tutoring Help?

5th Assignment
Class/Subject: ______________
Due Date:

Priority# ___
Estimate Time: ___
Actual Time: ___
❑ Test-Review Notes?
❑ Proofreading Help?
❑ Tutoring Help?

6th Assignment
Class/Subject: ______________
Due Date:

Priority# ___
Estimate Time: ___
Actual Time: ___
❑ Test-Review Notes?
❑ Proofreading Help?
❑ Tutoring Help?

At Home: My Study Schedule

7 Shift Study Schedule
45-Minute Study Periods and 15-Minute Breaks

Study Period 1
3-3:45   Subject: _________
15 Minute Study Break (stretch)

Study Period 2
4-4:45   Subject: _________
15 Minute Study Break (stretch)

Study Period 3
5-5:45   Subject:_________
15 Minute Study Break (stretch)

Study Period 4
6-6:45   Subject:_________
15 Minute Study Break (stretch)

Study Period 5
7-7:45   Subject:_________
15 Minute Study Break (stretch)

Study Period 6
8-8:45   Subject:_________
15 Minute Study Break (stretch)

Study Period 7
9-9:45   Subject: _________
15 Minutes: Pack Book Bag for Tomorrow

Regular Bedtime for Energy to Learn

Get Ready for Tomorrow!

❑ 1. Pack Book Bag
❑ 2. Check: Keys, School I.D., Wallet, Money, Pens and Pencils, Assignments
❑ 3. Check Weather (Umbrella? Snow Boots? Sunscreen?)
❑ 4. Q. What Will You Eat for Breakfast and Lunch Tomorrow?
❑ 5. Q. What Will You Wear to School Tomorrow?
❑ 6. Charge Electronic Devices (Computer, Cell Phone, and Watch)
❑ 7. Express Gratitude to Loved Ones (Hugs & Kisses, Love Note, Gift)
❑ 8. Brush & Floss Teeth
❑ 9. Set Alarm Clock

Set Priorities:

Priority #1
❑ Prepare EZ Study Snacks
e.g., Apple Slices, Banana,
Celery & Carrot Sticks

Priority #2
Q. What Time Is Dinner?

Priority #3
❑ Study Period #1
Study for Test!

Priority #4
❑ Study Period #2
What's Due Tomorrow?

Priority #5
❑ What's Due Next Week?

Priority #6
❑ Write Test-Review Notes
to Ace Tests:
1. Class Notes
2. Textbook Notes
3. Handout Notes

Priority #7
❑ Review Test-Review
Notes to Ace Tests

Priority #8
❑ Write Essays and
Research Reports
❑ Proofreading Help?

Priority #9
❑ Tutoring Help?

Priority #10
❑ Backup Computer

Priority #11
❑ Pack Book Bag

Priority #12
❑ Socialize with
Family & Friends
Time: 8-9 p.m.

Priority #13
❑ Stick to a Regular
Bedtime: 9-11 p.m.

My Daily Self-Care Journal

1. Practice Gratitude:
   I am grateful for...
----

2. Practice Positive Self-Talk:
   I am ...
----

3. Practice Meditation:
   Close your eyes for 1-5 minutes, and pay attention to your breathing.
   Focus your mind on your breathing to become centered and calmer.
----

4. My Healthy Food Energy Choices:

   Breakfast Energy: ____

   Lunch Energy: ____

   Dinner Energy: ____

   Study Snack Energy: _______________________________________

   Eat Whole Foods of Fresh Fruits and Vegetables. Minimize Processed Food and Junk Food.
----

5. My Budget: Save, Spend, and Splurge

Part 1. My Budget

Total Amount of Allowance & Earnings: $ ________ Budget

1. My Savings: Pay Yourself First! $ ________ Savings Bank Account

2. My Pocket Money $ ________ My Wallet

Part 2. My Expenses: Needs & Wants

1. Spend (My Needs): $ ________

2. Splurge (My Wants): $ ________

Total Expenses: $ ________

Part 3.
My Pocket Money Minus My Expenses = $ ________ Balance

6. My After-School Activity:

____

7. My Family Chores:

1.

2.

3.

____

8. A Random Act of Kindness:
I made a difference in someone else's life by...

____

9. Self-Reflection

❑ Great Day   ❑ Good Day   ❑ Bad Day

1. The Best Part of My Day:

----

2. The Worst Part of My Day:

----

3. How Can I Become a Better Person Tomorrow?

4. Did You Put **LOVE** Into Everything?

____

5. What Is the Stress Level at Home? _______ (#1-10)

6. What Is the Stress Level at School? _______ (#1-10)

____

Practice Building
Good Character Traits

1. Courage
2. Responsibility
3. Kindness
4. Optimisim
5. Loyalty
6. Confidence
7. Honesty
8. Compassion
9. Cooperation
10. Open-Minded
11. Keep Your Word
12. Respectful Communication
13. Courtesy
14. Fair Play

10. ENERGIZE

My Regular Bedtime for POPTART ENERGY Is: _______ p.m.

In Class: My Homework Assignments

Today's Date:

1st Assignment
Class/Subject: _____________
Due Date:

Priority# ___
Estimate Time: ___
Actual Time: ___
❑ Test-Review Notes?
❑ Proofreading Help?
❑ Tutoring Help?

2nd Assignment
Class/Subject: _____________
Due Date:

Priority# ___
Estimate Time: ___
Actual Time: ___
❑ Test-Review Notes?
❑ Proofreading Help?
❑ Tutoring Help?

3rd Assignment
Class/Subject: _____________
Due Date:

Priority# ___
Estimate Time: ___
Actual Time: ___
❑ Test-Review Notes?
❑ Proofreading Help?
❑ Tutoring Help?

4th Assignment
Class/Subject: _____________
Due Date:

Priority# ___
Estimate Time: ___
Actual Time: ___
❑ Test-Review Notes?
❑ Proofreading Help?
❑ Tutoring Help?

5th Assignment
Class/Subject: _____________
Due Date:

Priority# ___
Estimate Time: ___
Actual Time: ___
❑ Test-Review Notes?
❑ Proofreading Help?
❑ Tutoring Help?

6th Assignment
Class/Subject: _____________
Due Date:

Priority# ___
Estimate Time: ___
Actual Time: ___
❑ Test-Review Notes?
❑ Proofreading Help?
❑ Tutoring Help?

At Home: My Study Schedule

7 Shift Study Schedule
45-Minute Study Periods and 15-Minute Breaks

Study Period 1
3-3:45   Subject: __________
15 Minute Study Break (stretch)

Study Period 2
4-4:45   Subject: __________
15 Minute Study Break (stretch)

Study Period 3
5-5:45   Subject:__________
15 Minute Study Break (stretch)

Study Period 4
6-6:45   Subject:__________
15 Minute Study Break (stretch)

Study Period 5
7-7:45   Subject:__________
15 Minute Study Break (stretch)

Study Period 6
8-8:45   Subject:__________
15 Minute Study Break (stretch)

Study Period 7
9-9:45   Subject: __________
15 Minutes: Pack Book Bag for Tomorrow

Regular Bedtime for Energy to Learn

Get Ready for Tomorrow!

❑ 1. Pack Book Bag
❑ 2. Check: Keys, School I.D., Wallet, Money, Pens and Pencils, Assignments
❑ 3. Check Weather (Umbrella? Snow Boots? Sunscreen?)
❑ 4. Q. What Will You Eat for Breakfast and Lunch Tomorrow?
❑ 5. Q. What Will You Wear to School Tomorrow?
❑ 6. Charge Electronic Devices (Computer, Cell Phone, and Watch)
❑ 7. Express Gratitude to Loved Ones (Hugs & Kisses, Love Note, Gift)
❑ 8. Brush & Floss Teeth
❑ 9. Set Alarm Clock

Set Priorities:

Priority #1
❑ Prepare EZ Study Snacks
e.g., Apple Slices, Banana,
Celery & Carrot Sticks

Priority #2
Q. What Time Is Dinner?

Priority #3
❑ Study Period #1
Study for Test!

Priority #4
❑ Study Period #2
What's Due Tomorrow?

Priority #5
❑ What's Due Next Week?

Priority #6
❑ Write Test-Review Notes
to Ace Tests:
1. Class Notes
2. Textbook Notes
3. Handout Notes

Priority #7
❑ Review Test-Review
Notes to Ace Tests

Priority #8
❑ Write Essays and
Research Reports
❑ Proofreading Help?

Priority #9
❑ Tutoring Help?

Priority #10
❑ Backup Computer

Priority #11
❑ Pack Book Bag

Priority #12
❑ Socialize with
Family & Friends
Time: 8-9 p.m.

Priority #13
❑ Stick to a Regular
Bedtime: 9-11 p.m.

My Daily Self-Care Journal

1. Practice Gratitude:

   I am grateful for...

----

2. Practice Positive Self-Talk:

   I am ...

----

3. Practice Meditation:
   Close your eyes for 1-5 minutes, and pay attention to your breathing.
   Focus your mind on your breathing to become centered and calmer.

----

4. My Healthy Food Energy Choices:

   Breakfast Energy: ____

   Lunch Energy: ____

   Dinner Energy: ____

   Study Snack Energy: ____

   Eat Whole Foods of Fresh Fruits and Vegetables. Minimize Processed Food and Junk Food.

----

5. My Budget: Save, Spend, and Splurge

Part 1. My Budget

Total Amount of Allowance & Earnings: $ ________ Budget

1. My Savings: Pay Yourself First! $ ________ Savings Bank Account

2. My Pocket Money $ ________ My Wallet

Part 2. My Expenses: Needs & Wants

1. Spend (My Needs): $ ________

2. Splurge (My Wants): $ ________

Total Expenses: $ ________

Part 3.
My Pocket Money Minus My Expenses = $ ________ Balance

6. My After-School Activity:

____

7. My Family Chores:

    1.

    2.

    3.

____

8. A Random Act of Kindness:
   I made a difference in someone else's life by...

____

9. Self-Reflection

❑ Great Day   ❑ Good Day   ❑ Bad Day

1. The Best Part of My Day:

----

2. The Worst Part of My Day:

----

3. How Can I Become a Better Person Tomorrow?

4. Did You Put **LOVE** Into Everything?

____

5. What Is the Stress Level at Home? _______ (#1-10)

6. What Is the Stress Level at School? _______ (#1-10)

____

Practice Building
Good Character Traits

1. Courage
2. Responsibility
3. Kindness
4. Optimisim
5. Loyalty
6. Confidence
7. Honesty
8. Compassion
9. Cooperation
10. Open-Minded
11. Keep Your Word
12. Respectful Communication
13. Courtesy
14. Fair Play

10. ENERGIZE

My Regular Bedtime for POPTART ENERGY Is: ______ p.m.

In Class: My Homework Assignments

Today's Date:

1st Assignment
Class/Subject: ______________
Due Date:

Priority# ___
Estimate Time: ___
Actual Time: ___
❑ Test-Review Notes?
❑ Proofreading Help?
❑ Tutoring Help?

- -

2nd Assignment
Class/Subject: ______________
Due Date:

Priority# ___
Estimate Time: ___
Actual Time: ___
❑ Test-Review Notes?
❑ Proofreading Help?
❑ Tutoring Help?

- -

3rd Assignment
Class/Subject: ______________
Due Date:

Priority# ___
Estimate Time: ___
Actual Time: ___
❑ Test-Review Notes?
❑ Proofreading Help?
❑ Tutoring Help?

- -

4th Assignment
Class/Subject: ______________
Due Date:

Priority# ___
Estimate Time: ___
Actual Time: ___
❑ Test-Review Notes?
❑ Proofreading Help?
❑ Tutoring Help?

- -

5th Assignment
Class/Subject: ______________
Due Date:

Priority# ___
Estimate Time: ___
Actual Time: ___
❑ Test-Review Notes?
❑ Proofreading Help?
❑ Tutoring Help?

- -

6th Assignment
Class/Subject: ______________
Due Date:

Priority# ___
Estimate Time: ___
Actual Time: ___
❑ Test-Review Notes?
❑ Proofreading Help?
❑ Tutoring Help?

At Home: My Study Schedule

7 Shift Study Schedule
45-Minute Study Periods and 15-Minute Breaks

Study Period 1
3-3:45   Subject: __________
15 Minute Study Break (stretch)

Study Period 2
4-4:45   Subject: __________
15 Minute Study Break (stretch)

Study Period 3
5-5:45   Subject:__________
15 Minute Study Break (stretch)

Study Period 4
6-6:45   Subject:__________
15 Minute Study Break (stretch)

Study Period 5
7-7:45   Subject:__________
15 Minute Study Break (stretch)

Study Period 6
8-8:45   Subject:__________
15 Minute Study Break (stretch)

Study Period 7
9-9:45   Subject: __________
15 Minutes: Pack Book Bag for Tomorrow

Regular Bedtime for Energy to Learn

Get Ready for Tomorrow!

❑ 1. Pack Book Bag
❑ 2. Check: Keys, School I.D., Wallet, Money, Pens and Pencils, Assignments
❑ 3. Check Weather (Umbrella? Snow Boots? Sunscreen?)
❑ 4. Q. What Will You Eat for Breakfast and Lunch Tomorrow?
❑ 5. Q. What Will You Wear to School Tomorrow?
❑ 6. Charge Electronic Devices (Computer, Cell Phone, and Watch)
❑ 7. Express Gratitude to Loved Ones (Hugs & Kisses, Love Note, Gift)
❑ 8. Brush & Floss Teeth
❑ 9. Set Alarm Clock

Set Priorities:

Priority #1
❑ Prepare EZ Study Snacks
  e.g., Apple Slices, Banana,
  Celery & Carrot Sticks

Priority #2
Q. What Time Is Dinner?

Priority #3
❑ Study Period #1
  Study for Test!

Priority #4
❑ Study Period #2
  What's Due Tomorrow?

Priority #5
❑ What's Due Next Week?

Priority #6
❑ Write Test-Review Notes
  to Ace Tests:
  1. Class Notes
  2. Textbook Notes
  3. Handout Notes

Priority #7
❑ Review Test-Review
  Notes to Ace Tests

Priority #8
❑ Write Essays and
  Research Reports
❑ Proofreading Help?

Priority #9
❑ Tutoring Help?

Priority #10
❑ Backup Computer

Priority #11
❑ Pack Book Bag

Priority #12
❑ Socialize with
  Family & Friends
  Time: 8-9 p.m.

Priority #13
❑ Stick to a Regular
  Bedtime: 9-11 p.m.

My Daily Self-Care Journal

1. **Practice Gratitude:**
   I am grateful for...
----
2. **Practice Positive Self-Talk:**
   I am ...
----
3. **Practice Meditation:**
   Close your eyes for 1-5 minutes, and pay attention to your breathing.
   Focus your mind on your breathing to become centered and calmer.
----
4. **My Healthy Food Energy Choices:**

   Breakfast Energy: ___________________________________

   Lunch Energy: ___________________________________

   Dinner Energy: ___________________________________

   Study Snack Energy: ___________________________________

   Eat Whole Foods of Fresh Fruits and Vegetables. Minimize Processed Food and Junk Food.
----

5. My Budget: Save, Spend, and Splurge

Part 1. My Budget

Total Amount of Allowance & Earnings: $ ________ Budget

1. My Savings: Pay Yourself First! $ ________ Savings Bank Account

2. My Pocket Money $ ________ My Wallet

Part 2. My Expenses: Needs & Wants

1. Spend (My Needs): $ ________

2. Splurge (My Wants): $ ________

Total Expenses: $ ________

Part 3.
My Pocket Money Minus My Expenses = $ ________ Balance

6. My After-School Activity:

----

7. My Family Chores:

1.

2.

3.

----

8. A Random Act of Kindness:
I made a difference in someone else's life by...

----

9. Self-Reflection

❑ Great Day   ❑ Good Day   ❑ Bad Day

1. The Best Part of My Day:

----

2. The Worst Part of My Day:

----

3. How Can I Become a Better Person Tomorrow?

4. Did You Put **LOVE** Into Everything?

----

5. What Is the Stress Level at Home? _______ (#1-10)

6. What Is the Stress Level at School? _______ (#1-10)

Practice Building
Good Character Traits

1. Courage
2. Responsibility
3. Kindness
4. Optimisim
5. Loyalty
6. Confidence
7. Honesty
8. Compassion
9. Cooperation
10. Open-Minded
11. Keep Your Word
12. Respectful Communication
13. Courtesy
14. Fair Play

10. ENERGIZE

My Regular Bedtime for POPTART ENERGY Is: _______ p.m.

SMARTGRADES Grade Tracker

Grades and % of Grade

Class:

Tests/Quizzes:

Essays/Papers:

Projects:

Final Grade:

Good Grades Deserve Great Rewards:

Class:

Tests/Quizzes:

Essays/Papers:

Projects:

Final Grade:

Good Grades Deserve Great Rewards:

Class:

Tests/Quizzes:

Essays/Papers:

Projects:

Final Grade:

Good Grades Deserve Great Rewards:

Class:

Tests/Quizzes:

Essays/Papers:

Projects:

Final Grade:

Good Grades Deserve Great Rewards:

Good Grades Deserve Great Rewards

Class:

Tests/Quizzes:

Essays/Papers:

Projects:

Final Grade:

Good Grades Deserve Great Rewards:

Class:

Tests/Quizzes:

Essays/Papers:

Projects:

Final Grade:

Good Grades Deserve Great Rewards:

Class:

Tests/Quizzes:

Essays/Papers:

Projects:

Final Grade:

Good Grades Deserve Great Rewards:

Class:

Tests/Quizzes:

Essays/Papers:

Projects:

Final Grade:

Good Grades Deserve Great Rewards:

My Teacher Contacts

Class:
Teacher:
Office Hours:
Phone Number:
Email:
Teacher's Pet Peeves:
Ask Teacher for a Recommendation:

Class:
Teacher:
Office Hours:
Phone Number:
Email:
Teacher's Pet Peeves:
Ask Teacher or a Recommendation:

Class:
Teacher:
Office Hours:
Phone Number:
Email:
Teacher's Pet Peeves:
Ask Teacher for a Recommendation:

Class:
Teacher:
Office Hours:
Phone Number:
Email:
Teacher's Pet Peeves:
Ask Teacher for a Recommendation:

Class:
Teacher:
Office Hours:
Phone Number:
Email:
Teacher's Pet Peeves:
Ask Teacher for a Recommendation:

Class:
Teacher:
Office Hours:
Phone Number:
Email:
Teacher's Pet Peeves:
Ask Teacher for a Recommendation:

My Study Buddies

Class:
Study Buddy:
Phone Number:
E-Mail:
Birthday:
Interests:

Class:
Study Buddy:
Phone Number:
E-Mail:
Birthday:
Interests:

Class:
Study Buddy:
Phone Number:
E-Mail:
Birthday:
Interests:

Class:
Study Buddy:
Phone Number:
E-Mail:
Birthday:
Interests:

Class:
Study Buddy:
Phone Number:
E-Mail:
Birthday:
Interests:

Class:
Study Buddy:
Phone Number:
E-Mail:
Birthday:
Interests:

PHOTON'S
10 Facts of Academic Success

In-Class

1. School Is a Restaurant and Facts Are on the Menu. Food Is for the Body and Facts Are for the Brain!

2. All Teachers Say the Same Things:
   1. Read a Chapter
   2. Write a Paper
   3. Solve a Problem
   4. Study for a Test

At-Home

3. Set Up a Comfortable Study Room: Desk, Chair, and Lighting

4. Your **REPORT CARD** Tells You About the Schoolwork You Do at Home:
   1. Math: Homework, Study for Test
   2. English: Read Chapter, Write Paper, Study for Test

USE SMARTGRADES SUCCESS STRATEGY

5. Practice Active Reading: As You Read, Make **Test-Review Notes**

6. **"Writing Is Rewriting"**: Read, Edit, Revise, Repeat! (10X)

7. Everyone Needs Proofreading Help! Find a Pair of Fresh Eyes! Ask Family or Friends! Use **READ ALOUD** Software!

8. Ace Your Research Papers: Use **SMARTGRADES Essay Success Strategy** Read Book: EVERY DAY AN EASY A! (everydayaneasya.com)

9. Ace Your Test! Use **SMARTGRADES Test Success Strategy** Read Book: TOTAL RECALL: ACE EVERY TEST EVERY TIME

10. Follow Your Passion, Fulfill Your Potential and Find Your Place in the World!

PHOTON'S
Postive Self-Talk Affirmations

Choose a positive self-talk from this list, until you can write your own positive self-talk affirmation:

Write Your Own Daily Positive Affirmation:

1. I am filled with light, love, and peace!

2. I have the strength to make my dreams come true!

3. Anything I set my mind to, I can do!

4. I treat myself with kindness and respect!

5. I am my own best friend and cheerleader!

6. I grow in strength with every forward step I take!

7. I believe in and trust myself!

8. I give myself permission to shine!

9. I open my mind to endless opportunities...

10. I am very proud of myself for even daring to try!

11. Each decision I make creates new opportunities!

WWW.PHOTONSUPERHERO.COM

PHOTON'S
22 Spiritual Illuminations

1. LIFE Over Death

2. STRENGTH Over Weakness

3. DEED over Sin

4. LOVE over Hatred

5. TRUTH over Lie

6. COURAGE over Fear

7. OPTIMISM over Pessimism

8. SHARING over Selfishness

9. PRAISE over Criticism

10. LOYALTY over Abandonment

11. RESPONSIBILITY over Blame

12. GRATITUDE over envy

13. REWARD over Punishment

14. ALLIES over Enemies

15. CREATION over Destruction

16. EDUCATION over Ignorance

17. COOPERATION over Competition

18. FREEDOM over Oppression

19. COMPASSION over Indifference

20. FORGIVENESS over Revenge

21. PEACE over War

22. JOY over Suffering

WWW.PHOTONSUPERHERO.COM

PHOTON
EVERY DAY AN EASY A

Dark Ages Despair.
PHOTON Is Here.

Enlightenment Is Her Destiny.
World Peace Is Her Legacy.

Nurture the Human Brain.
Keep Planet Earth Sane.

Ignorance Is the Enemy.
Education Is the Remedy.

SMARTGRADES
SCHOOL NOTEBOOKS
Will Prevail.
No Student Will Fail.

Students and Educators Are a Team.
Good Grades Become Grand Dreams.

Ignorance Is Bitter Not Bliss.
I Seal this Promise with a Kiss.

BUY NOW!
AMAZON 2 DAY SHIP
GLOBAL BOOKSTORES

EVERY DAY AN EASY A
TOTAL RECALL
YOUR STUDY ROOM IS UNDER NEW MANAGEMENT
SMARTGRADES SCHOOL NOTEBOOKS AND ACADEMIC PLANNER

EVERYBODY IS SOMEBODY SPECIAL
www.BooksNotBombs.com

PHOTON
SUPERHERO of EDUCATION ®

EVERY DAY AN EASY A

3 Editions: Elementary, High School, College

ACE EVERY TEST EVERY TIME
All Global Bookstores

www.BooksNotBombs.com
EVERYBODY IS SOMEBODY SPECIAL

---

1 Minute Time Management Class
10 Steps to Success

EVERY DAY AN EASY A ©All Rights Reserved 2010.

Step 1 ❏
Make a Daily Action Plan
Write Down Your Big Goals

Step 2 ❏
Set Your Priorities
Urgent, Important, Low, and Optional

Step 3 ❏
Breakdown Your Dreams
Breakdown Big Goal into Smaller Steps
List Steps Necessary to Complete Big Goal

Step 4 ❏
Divide and Conquer
Take Baby Steps Toward Reaching Goal
Crawl. Walk. Fly. Soar...

Step 5 ❏
Use Time Logs: Estimated Vs. Actual Time
e.g., Estimate Time for Lunch: 1 Hour
Actual Time: 20 Minutes
40 Minutes for Errands: Bank, Post Office, Store

Step 6 ❏
Life Is a Bumpy Road
Make Time for Delays, Detours,
Distractions, and Disappointments
e.g., Copier Runs Out of Toner and Paper

Step 7 ❏
Use Checkboxes to Keep Track of Completed Tasks

Step 8 ❏
Review and Refine Daily Action Plan
Pay Attention to Strengths and Weaknesses

Step 9 ❏
Celebrate Your Success
Celebrate Job Well Done with Daily Reward

Step 10 ❏
EVERY DAY AN EASY A
www.everydayaneasya.com